GOOD NEWS

THAT TRANSFORMS

The Genuine Gospel for an Artificial World

✢

DALE L. STOLL

RESTORATION PRESS
Bristol, Indiana

© Dale L. Stoll and Radical Restoration Ministries, LLC

Printed in the United States of America

ISBN 0-9773643-1-3

Library of Congress Control Number 2005934930

All Scripture quotations in this publication, except where noted, are from the HOLY BIBLE, NEW INTERNATIONAL VERSION® NIV® Copyright © 1973, 1978, 1984 by International Bible Society. All rights reserved.

Scripture quotations marked "NKJV"® are taken from the New King James Version®. Copyright © 1982 by Thomas Nelson, Inc. Used by permission. All rights reserved.

Scripture quotations marked NLT are taken from the *Holy Bible*, New Living Translation, copyright © 1996. Used by permission of Tyndale House Publishers, Inc., Carol Stream, Illinois 60188. All rights reserved.

Scripture quotations marked *The Message* are taken from *The Message* by Eugene H. Peterson, copyright (c) 1993, 1994, 1995, 1996, 2000, 2001, 2002. Used by permission of NavPress Publishing Group. All rights reserved.

CONTENTS

Acknowledgments 7

Introduction 9

Chapter 1: How About Some Good News? 15

Chapter 2: What Is the Good News? 37

Chapter 3: The Kingdom of God 57

Chapter 4: The Good News of the Kingdom 79

Chapter 5: The Process of Transformation 99

Chapter 6: Taking Hold of the Good News 125

Chapter 7: Sharing the Good News With Others 145

Chapter 8: Good News for Daily Living 161

Epilogue 185

Notes 189

Bibliography 195

About the Author 199

ACKNOWLEDGMENTS

Very little, if anything, of significance is accomplished alone in the kingdom of God. We are each part of Christ's new community, the Church, and the gifts and abilities of one add to those of another to accomplish the work God assigns to us. So it has been with this book.

So many people have impacted my life for the better and have contributed to this book in one way or another. It would be impossible to recognize them all. However, there are some who stand out in the crowd.

First, there is Gwen, my wonderful wife of 36 years. Without the unselfish giving of herself to the care of our children and her faithful, never-ending support, I would not have attempted this project. I have no adequate words to describe what she means to me.

Then there are Harold Bauman and Keith Yoder, my overseers, mentors, and friends. These two brothers have encouraged, supported, challenged, and corrected me when needed—and I am a better person for it. I long for every minister to experience the kind of oversight and loving accountability they have extended to me over many years.

I am also very grateful for the support and encouragement expressed by all the sisters and brothers who partner with me in Radical Restoration Ministries. They have read my writings and offered helpful suggestions over the years that have always stimulated my thinking. Their feedback on the first draft of this book resulted in a final product that is more comprehensive in scope, and will likely be more helpful to its readers.

Finally, two people who worked directly with me on this book have greatly enhanced the end result. Harriet Miller has been responsible for the cover design, artwork, layout and production. My editor, Mark Garratt, has made countless improvements to my writing. I am very grateful for their invaluable assistance.

May God be glorified, and may the work of the kingdom go forth as together we serve Jesus, our Lord and Savior and soon-coming King!

INTRODUCTION

We, who come last, desire to see the first things and wish to return to them insofar as God enables us. We are like people who have come to a house that has been burnt down and try to find the original foundations. This is more difficult in that the ruins are grown over with all sorts of growths, and many think that these growths are the foundation, and say, 'This is the foundation' and 'This is the way in which all must go,' and others repeat it after them. So that in the novelties that have grown up they think to have found the foundation, whereas they have found something quite different from, and contrary to, the true foundation.
(Peter Cheltschizki, Bohemia, 1440[1])

In July of 1979, I began my first and only pastorate in a local church. In many ways, I was considered a successful pastor. The church grew from about 25 to over 275 in worship attendance. We completed a building program as we "enlarged the place of our tent" (Isa. 54:2)—the slogan for our building campaign. Moreover, I survived as pastor for over 22 years in the same place! Now that's surely success! Or is it? How *do* we measure success in the church? That's a question that has stayed with me over the years.

In the fall of 1985, I first read a report by George Gallup, Jr. reflecting the results of the Gallup Organization's polling on religious issues over the previous half-century. Part of that report read as follows:

Certain basic themes emerge from the mass of survey data collected over the period of five decades—themes that probably apply not only to the 50-year history of scientific polling, but to the history of the nation:
- The widespread appeal or popularity of religion
- The gap between belief and commitment; between high religiosity and low ethics
- The glaring lack of knowledge
- What would appear to be a failure, in part, of organized religion to make a difference in society in terms of morality and ethics
- The superficiality of faith.[2]

Around that same time, I read another report, one that I can no longer document, but one that I will not forget. In essence, it stated that, concerning the behaviors of lying and cheating, there was little or no significant difference between the churched and the unchurched population. These two reports started a quest for me that has continued to this day. *Why?* Why do we see this "gap between belief and commitment?"

In the years since these original polling results were released, Gallup, George Barna, and others have consistently reported this huge gap between belief and behavior within the church. In Gallup's words, "When our nation's four to five hundred thousand clergy address their congregations each week, they face people whose choices contradict their values...(they) preach to boomers who believe in angels but cheat on taxes, college students who pray but regularly get drunk."[3] And I didn't have to read the surveys to see this discrepancy: I saw it in many of the people I loved and served—and too often in my own life.

As I grappled with these observations and questions over the last 20 years, I arrived at two conclusions. First, the only reliable measure of success for the church must be transformed lives, nothing else. Church growth won't cut it. The number and quality of programs offered don't tell us what we need to know. Average church attendance doesn't. The number of small groups doesn't. The number of baptisms doesn't give us a definitive answer. These may all be indicators to one degree or another, but only transformed lives truly tell the story—because only God can transform a life. We can produce just about every other statistic on our own—if we are gifted and smart enough—but we can't transform a life.

What is a transformed life? To transform is "to change markedly the appearance or form of; to change the nature, function, or condition of; convert."[4] A transformed life, then, is one that has experienced a change in nature that results in a visible change of behavior. It is a life that is becoming more like Christ's. And when a life is truly being transformed, everyone close to that person knows it.

Now, if transformation in nature and behavior in order to look more like Jesus is the measure of success for the church, then, given the statistics above, we must certainly question how successful we have been. I concluded that my 22 years were not that successful. That doesn't mean nothing good happened. A lot of good things were happening—but not a lot of lives were being transformed, according to our definition.

In October of 2001, I resigned my pastorate, to give my full time to the pursuit of these questions and to overseeing several other pastors. I can't go back and change the last 25 years, but I can learn from them and help others go beyond me in the years ahead.

These years have brought me to my second conclusion: Problems at the most foundational level have produced these results. And, further, we need to hear the words of Dallas Willard. Addressing the poor overall result we have experienced, he raises a good question: "Should we not at least consider the possibility that this poor result is not in spite of what we teach and how we teach, but precisely because of it?[5]

As Peter Cheltschizki wrote over 500 years ago, there are "novelties" that have grown over and obscured the true foundation, and now are believed to *be* the foundation. Yet, they are actually "quite different from, and contrary to, the true foundation." This word is at least as applicable today as it was when it was written in 1440. These "novelties" today go as deep as the very message we have proclaimed as the gospel, the good news. That's what this book is about.

In our well-intentioned efforts to simplify the gospel and to make it "relevant" to our culture, we have ended up with several versions of the good news that are no longer that good—they no longer have the power to transform. I call these artificial gospels. The result of these artificial gospels is aptly expressed by Gallup:

> Contemporary spirituality can resemble a grab bag of random experiences that does little more than promise to make our eyes mist up or our heart warm. We need perspective to separate the junk food from the wholesome, the faddish from the truly transforming.[6]

That doesn't mean they do not contain truth; it just means they are no longer the original. They are manmade—that's the definition of artificial. We have taken portions of God's truth and packaged them in ways that change the overall message. Artificial does not mean all bad. Artificial light is a good thing—it enabled me to work on this manuscript many nights long after dark. But my farmer son needs real sunlight to grow his crops.

Artificial gospels have a reciprocal relationship with the artificial cultures that dominate our Western world. They are both produced by, and then end up producing, artificial cultures. Again, artificial cultures are not all bad—they just fall short of what God intended when he created life.

In this book, we will look first at these artificial cultures and gospels, and then go back to the Bible to recover the originals—the "kingdom of God," and the "gospel of the kingdom" proclaimed by Jesus and the early church. This is the *Good News That Transforms*.

We will then look at how this good news connects with our lives to produce the transformation that we desire, and how we actually take hold of this good news. Finally, we will suggest a paradigm for sharing this valuable gift with others, and offer some thoughts on how to cultivate the new life it brings.

I wrote this book with two audiences in mind. First, I wrote it for those who have already committed their lives to Jesus as their Lord and Savior, yet need a better understanding of the "kingdom of God" and of "the good news of the kingdom" that Jesus proclaimed. After all, he talked more about the kingdom of God than any other subject. Does it not behoove us, then, to make sure we understand what he was talking about?

Secondly, I wrote this book as a resource for this first group to pass on to—and discuss with—their seeker friends. Most people who come to faith in Jesus and trust him with their lives are led there by friends who care enough to share their lives with them. This book can simply be used as a way of introducing Jesus and his message to your friends in the context of your everyday relationships.

Finally, my prayer as you read these pages comes from Eugene Peterson's paraphrase of Romans 12:1-2 in *The Message*:

> So here's what I want you to do, God helping you: Take your everyday, ordinary life—your sleeping, eating, going-to-work, and walking-around life—and

place it before God as an offering. Embracing what God does for you is the best thing you can do for him. Don't become so well-adjusted to your culture that you fit into it without even thinking. Instead, fix your attention on God. You'll be changed from the inside out. Readily recognize what he wants from you, and quickly respond to it. Unlike the culture around you, always dragging you down to its level of immaturity, God brings the best out of you, develops well-formed maturity in you.

May we think before we just fit in. May we fix our attention on God and be changed from the inside out. And, may we together be "transformed into his likeness with ever-increasing glory, which comes from the Lord, who is the Spirit" (2 Cor. 3:18).

Chapter 1

How About Some Good News?

After John was put in prison, Jesus went into Galilee, proclaiming the good news of God. 'The time has come,' he said. 'The kingdom of God is near. Repent and believe the good news!'" (Mark 1:14-15)

He is before all things, and in him all things hold together. (Colossians 1:17)

Seldom a day passes without something popping up on my computer with "good news" for me. Recently this gem flashed on my screen: "Congratulations! You have been selected to receive a free 42-inch Plasma TV!"

Wow! Those things cost thousands of dollars! That's good news for sure—or is it? I decided to go to the website to take a look around. First I had to go through a number of pages of "special offers" and indicate if I was interested or not. Since I was only going for the "free 42-inch Plasma TV," I indicated "Not interested!" to all the offers. Then I came to pages where I had to buy into at least one special offer from each page before going on to the next one—to eventually qualify for my free TV after who knows how many more special offers!

That's where I quit. Is it good news if I must commit myself to something I do not need and cannot really afford in the long run, just to get a "free TV" in the short run? I have no doubt that anyone going all the way through the process and qualifying for the free TV would end up paying more than the cost of the TV eventually. Everyone likes good news—but not everything that claims to be good news really is!

Six Spiritual Needs
But how about some genuine good news—something that goes much deeper than free plasma TV's or laptops or digital cameras or other electronic gadgets? In 1992, George H. Gallup, Jr. of the Gallup polling organization wrote of "Six Spiritual Needs of Americans," based on the results of Gallup's polling over the years:

1. To have a sense of community and deeper relationships.
2. To believe life is meaningful and has a purpose.
3. To be appreciated and be respected.
4. To be listened to and be heard.
5. To feel that one is growing in the faith.
6. To have practical help in developing a mature faith.[1]

Consider these six needs. are they currently being met in your life? Would it be good news if they were? Let's think for a moment about just the second of these six. Do you believe "life is meaningful and has a purpose?" If so, are you *experiencing* it that way? If not, where would you look to find meaning and purpose for your life?

Cultural Differences
What we see as genuine, true, and valuable varies from one culture to another *and* determines where we tend to look for

meaning and purpose in life. If we understand cultural differences, we will have a much better chance of understanding people living in another culture—not to mention a much better chance of building healthy relationships with them. But to understand these differences, we must first understand how cultures are defined.

Culture is defined as "the set of shared attitudes, values, goals, and practices that characterize a unit of society."[2] But it's helpful to further break this basic definition down into two different levels, as not all cultural differences are equally significant. *Primary cultures* are defined more by the "shared attitudes and values," while *subcultures* are defined more by "goals and practices." When crossing cultures, differing goals and practices may cause more initial cultural shock. However, as you get to know people better in the different culture, you may find that at the level of worldview and fundamental values, you have more in common with them than you do your next door neighbor!

A concrete example will help us understand this. Thirty years ago I met a Nigerian man who was a fellow student in the Bible college I was attending. He and his wife ended up living with my family, and we became very close friends over the nine years they lived here in the United States before returning home in 1984.

When my wife, Gwen, and I made our first trip to visit them in 1988, we encountered a host of cultural differences. They dressed differently than us—much more colorful. Their language was different. They ate differently than us—yam and rice rather than meat and potatoes, *and* with a lot more hot pepper! Time just did not have the same meaning that it had to us—the most difficult adjustment for me. When I lead a meeting, I have a goal of starting and ending on time. I don't think that ever crosses their minds!

But once we got beyond these secondary differences, we found that, at a primary level, we shared the same basic worldview and value system as did our Christian sisters and brothers there. Consequently, it was not difficult to establish relationships at a deep level, ones that have continued to grow with each return trip we have made.

In fact, we shared the same primary culture, the culture of the kingdom of God, with the same "attitudes and values." Within that primary culture, we represented two different subcultures, with many different "goals and practices." And yet, when it came to the question of where we look to find meaning and purpose for life, we were much closer to these sisters and brothers than to many of our neighbors back home.

Three Primary Cultures

In today's Western world we find three primary cultures: modern, postmodern, and—in a few places—the culture of the kingdom of God. These are the three primary cultures because they differ at the level of fundamental worldview and values, as we have already discussed. For this reason, they attempt to find meaning and purpose in life in very different places.

Modern Culture

Throughout the modern cultural era—from the beginning of the Industrial Revolution through the middle of the 20th century—many people looked to science and the material world to bring meaning and purpose to life. Science would answer every question and solve every problem, and material things would bring happiness and meaning and purpose.

We must acknowledge that we have all benefited much from the rise of the scientific method. For example, who has not benefited from the advances of medical science? And what about technology? How different our lives would be today without computers! Without refrigerators! Without microwave ovens! And how would we even survive without our cell phones?

But we must also understand the difference between scientific method and scientism. Scientific method is exactly that—a method for discovering the truth about something. Scientism, on the other hand, is not a method but a philosophy. Scientism says that science is the *only* way to any and all truth. It operates in a closed system, with no place for God or anything supernatural. But the reality was that scientism promised more than it could deliver, which led to a reaction.

Postmodern Culture
The 1950's was a time of great optimism: World War II—the war to end all wars—was over! Soldiers came home and families were reunited. All those factories that had been supplying the weapons and machines of war could be returned to producing all the things that people wanted to buy. The greatest consumer push in history was underway, and everything about the future looked rosy—or did it?

About the same time, a lot of young people began to realize that many questions, especially ones pertaining to meaning and purpose—in spite of our prosperity—were still left unanswered. They began to react to the world and the ways of their parents, and the cultural upheaval of the 60's was born. Although its roots are much older and other factors no doubt contributed to its rise, this rebellion against modernism that developed over the last half of the 20th century has come to be known as postmodernism.

In modern culture, truth was objective, concrete, something to be discovered in the lab. In postmodern culture, truth is simply a socially-constructed reality, as abstract and subjective as are people and their cultures.

The materialism of modern culture tended to either squeeze God totally out of the picture, or confine him to a religious realm considered totally irrelevant to everyday life. You can take God to church on Sunday, just don't try to take him to school or work with you! Postmodern culture is more likely to see God in everything—defined, of course, as you choose! In postmodern culture, you don't look for meaning and purpose somewhere else—you look inside your own head and create it for yourself.

Actually, modernism and postmodernism are two opposite expressions of the same human-centered worldview. As Oz Guinness has pointed out, "Postmodernism, in fact, is the mirror image of modernism and is born of its deficiencies. It is therefore equally confused and equally confusing, but in a reverse way."[3] As human-centered systems of thought, they are both ditches alongside the road of God's truth, just on opposite sides.

Kingdom Culture

But we don't need to be confused: there is an alternative! We are not stuck with choosing between modern and postmodern culture when looking for meaning and purpose in life. Jesus came to this earth speaking about an alternative culture, one he called, "the kingdom of God."

In this kingdom culture, God is neither squeezed out nor relegated to the sidelines, nor is he defined by and answerable to you ... or me ... or anyone else. He is the *God Who Is There* to use a title from Francis Schaeffer—there at the center of all that is genuine.

Truth is neither limited to what can be verified in the lab, nor is it whatever you decide it to be. Ultimately, truth is revealed by the *God Who Is There* as a person—a real, historical person who walked the face of this earth just as you and I do today. His name is Jesus.

In this alternative culture, meaning and purpose are found in a living relationship with the Living God. And, this relationship is one that impacts *all* of life as we "grow in the grace and knowledge of our Lord and Savior Jesus Christ" (2 Pet. 3:18).

Unfortunately, we must address a major problem at this point. As we will see, while God clearly intended for Christians to experience fullness of life in a kingdom culture, it is also clear that many settle for less. For many Christians in our Western world, life is lived simply as a subculture of either modern or postmodern culture. Most have never once thought of Christianity as a distinct primary culture. Howard Snyder defines the difference between Christianity as primary culture and Christianity as subculture very well:

> A subculture is in fundamental agreement with the dominant culture on major issues and values, but has distinct secondary values and characteristics. By contrast, a counterculture is in tension with the dominant culture at the level of fundamental values, even though it may share many secondary characteristics with that culture. The church functions as a subculture, not as a counterculture, when it fails to oppose the dominant culture at those points where the culture pays allegiance to alien gods rather than to the Kingdom of God.[4]

Both George Gallup's research and, more recently, that of George Barna point clearly to Christianity as a subculture rather than a counterculture or alternative primary culture. Our lifestyles are basically the same as our non-Christian neighbors, which mean we are living out the same set of fundamental values. Often this has happened because we have done exactly what Paul warned the Roman Christians about centuries ago:

> Don't become so well-adjusted to your culture that you fit into it without even thinking. Instead, fix your attention on God. You'll be changed from the inside out. Readily recognize what he wants from you, and quickly respond to it. Unlike the culture around you, always dragging you down to its level of immaturity, God brings the best out of you, develops well-formed maturity in you. (Rom. 12:2, *The Message*)

John R. W. Stott summarizes the problem: "If the church realistically accepted Jesus' standards and values and lived by them, it would be the alternative society he always intended it to be, and would offer to the world an authentic Christian counterculture."[5]

Understanding the difference between Christianity as a subculture and Christianity as an alternative primary culture is at the heart of what this book is about. And there is no way to understand and appreciate this difference without getting down to the very foundational question: "What is the *genuine* good news?"

Three primary cultures. Three different answers to the question of meaning and purpose. But which one provides an answer that will actually hold up in real life? To answer that question, we must look deeper.

The Great Divide

It is important to understand these different cultures. Otherwise, we have no real way to communicate with them. People in all three cultures may use the same words and mean something very different. Take for example the word, *god*. A modern person may use *god* simply as the way weak people explain what they don't understand. A postmodern person may tell you that *god* means whatever you want it to mean. Truly, as Francis Schaeffer has written, "No word is as meaningless as the word *god* until content is put to it."[6] For a Christian living in a kingdom culture, God is not just a word, but both an infinite and personal God. In Hebrew, his name is *Yahweh*.

If we want to truly understand these three different cultures we must look deep below the surface. We must look to the roots from which they grow. We must think deeply rather than just at a superficial level. Unfortunately, it is not a popular thing today to *muse*—to think deeply. It is much more popular to *a·muse* ourselves—to not think. This is a major problem in our time, as people who refuse to think will, sooner or later, end up deceived.

The Real Question
The ultimate divide between modernism and postmodernism on the one side and the kingdom of God on the other is one identified long ago: either there is a God who created human beings in his image, or the human race has created god in our image. The question is *not*, "Which came first, the chicken or the egg?" The real question is, "Which came first, God or the human race?"

As far back as 1841, Ludwig Feuerbach recognized the significance of this question:

> If human nature is the highest nature to man, then practically also the highest and first law must be the love of man to man. *Homo homini Deus est* (Man's God is Man):—this is the great practical principle:—this is the axis on which revolves the history of the world.[7]

While Feuerbach's conclusion was wrong, he was right about the importance of the question. *How we answer the God question is truly "the axis on which revolves the history of the world."* It also determines what is genuine and what is artificial.

The Genuine and The Artificial

Something that is genuine is "true and actual; not imaginary, alleged, or ideal ... Genuine and authentic; not artificial or spurious."[8] On the other hand, something that is artificial is "Made by human beings; produced rather than natural; Brought about or caused by sociopolitical or other human-generated forces or influences; Made in imitation of something natural; simulated; Not genuine or natural."[9]

That which is created by God is genuine; that which is manmade is artificial. For those who believe that God preceded the human race, this is not hard to accept. God created the real world, including the human race. As we will see later, God intended to partner with us in the development of that creation.

But once you start with the human race apart from the genuine Creator God, everything becomes fuzzy in our thinking, as we shall also see. Eventually, we get to the place where nothing is clear—no true and false, no right and wrong, as there is no real basis for determining this. There is no longer the possibility of thesis and antithesis, like true and false, right and wrong. Everything is relative. It was the German philosopher Hegel (1770-1831) who first developed this idea that all opposing ideas can be resolved through synthesis, an idea which opened the doorway to the relativism of postmodern culture.

Jesus, however, thought differently: He said "He who is not with me is against me" (Matt. 12:30), and "Whoever is not against us is for us" (Mk. 9:40). He left no neutral ground—no room for synthesis in this case. Anyone who hears the truth and refuses to recognize Jesus for who he is has, by default, rejected him.

The same is true concerning what is at the center of this world. If Feuerbach was right, then *god* is artificial—not genuine or natural, just a manmade idea. However, if he was wrong and God is real, then Feuerbach's *view of the world* is artificial. It is an imitation of the genuine thing. There is no neutral ground here either.

The Reality of God
When it comes to evidence for the reality of God, we are not left to make a blind leap of faith. There is much evidence that God is real. First, Paul wrote that creation itself was sufficient evidence for us to give glory to God:

> Acts of human mistrust and wrongdoing and lying accumulate, as people try to put a shroud over truth. But the basic reality of God is plain enough. Open your eyes and there it is! By taking a long and thoughtful look at what God has created, people have always been able to see what their eyes as such can't see: eternal power, for instance, and the mystery of his divine being. So nobody has a good excuse. (Rom. 1:18-20, *The Message*).

Today, more and more good science (that which is not bound up in scientism) is revealing the truth of Paul's words: behind this world in which we live is an Intelligent Designer—the Creator God. It is beyond the scope of this book to document all of this. I simply commend to you *How Now Shall We Live* by Charles Colson and Nancy Pearcey. It will give you a clear picture of the abundant and growing scientific evidence that supports a God-centered and biblical view of the world.

Beyond this general revelation of God in creation, Jesus came to this earth as a real human being who walked the face of this earth just like you and me. He said he was sent by God, whom he called "Father"—one as personal and real as he was. Furthermore, he claimed to reveal the character of Creator God:

> Anyone who has seen me has seen the Father....I have revealed you to those whom you gave me out of the world. They were yours; you gave them to me and they have obeyed your word. Now they know that everything you have given me comes from you. (Jn. 14:9; 17:6,7)

God is real. More than that, he has revealed himself to us. To use the title from another of Francis Schaeffer's books, *He Is There and He Is Not Silent*. The words of the Bible are very clear:

> In the past God spoke to our forefathers through the prophets at many times and in various ways, but in these last days he has spoken to us by his Son, whom he appointed heir of all things, and through whom he made the universe. The Son is the radiance of God's glory and the exact representation of his being, sustaining all things by his powerful word. After he had provided purification for sins, he sat down at the right hand of the Majesty in heaven. (Heb. 1:1-3)

Furthermore, before leaving this earth to return to Father God, Jesus gave his followers words of great comfort:

> I will not leave you as orphans; I will come to you.... the Counselor, the Holy Spirit, whom the Father will

send in my name, will teach you all things and will remind you of everything I have said to you. (Jn. 14: 18,26)

The infinite and personal God who first created this world continues to be present with us today by the Holy Spirit. The Holy Spirit convicts us of sin, grants us grace to change, and empowers us for service in the kingdom of God. This experience of the Holy Spirit in the lives of millions of Believers is another evidence of the reality of God.

Beginning with Abraham, God began calling out a people through whom he would reveal himself to the world he created. In the Old Testament we have the record of that historical revelation. In the New Testament, we have the continuing record, culminating in God's supreme revelation in the person of Jesus, "the exact representation of his being." God has been, and is, faithful in revealing himself to us. To ignore this revelation has serious consequences, as we will see below.

Integrated or Fragmented?

From ancient times the human race has known there is more to this world than just the material world around us. But what is it? And whatever it is, how does it relate to what we see and touch?

The Ancient Greek philosopher Plato (428-347 BC) believed there existed a perfect *world of forms*. He believed everything we see in this material world to be an imperfect copy of the real form. For example, he thought a physical horse that he could see was an imperfect copy of the perfect form of a horse in the unseen world of forms.

Plato's student Aristotle eventually said, in effect, "Maybe there is, maybe there isn't." Even if there is a world of forms, we have no way of knowing for sure—we can't bridge the gap.

Therefore, it's not worth thinking about. His solution was to effectively ignore anything not material.

Plato and Aristotle were both partially right, yet both very wrong. As Plato thought, there is another world—a spiritual world. As Aristotle thought, we have no way to bridge the gap to know for sure. But what he didn't know was that the gap had been and would be bridged from the other side, as we shall see later.

A spiritual world and a material world. A supernatural realm and a natural realm. In philosophical terms, the realm of universals and the realm of particulars; or, the realm of the nonrational and the rational. Whatever the language used, throughout history the problem has been the same: how to keep these two realms of life together—*how to keep life integrated*.

When these two dimensions of life are torn apart, we end up with a fragmented and artificial version of the life God intended. Francis Schaeffer has outlined the history of this problem perhaps better than anyone else. He speaks of these two realms as the "upper story" and the "lower story," and the line that separates them as a "line of despair."[10] We will use Schaeffer's upper story and lower story terminology throughout this book to refer to the spiritual realm and the material, or physical realm, respectively.

Fragmented Worlds

Actually, neither modernism nor postmodernism are either *modern* or *postmodern*—they are both current expressions of the ancient ideas of Aristotle and Plato. Both are the result of following Feuerbach's conclusion that "man's god is man," and then trying to work out a solution to the deep problems of life working only from ourselves.

Modern culture followed Aristotle in ruling out the "upper story" and dealing only with the lower. But as Jean-Paul

Sarte (1905-1980), Albert Camus (1913-1960) and others discovered, to try to live only in the lower story is absurd—life without an upper story has no meaning in itself, and no one can really live this way.

But if there really is no God in the upper story—or if there is but he has never revealed himself in the lower story—then the only solution to the despair of living in an absurd world is to try to bridge the gap ourselves. This is the "leap of faith" that Soren Kierkegaard (1813-1855) and others who followed him spoke about. With a "leap of faith" you create your own upper story.

We should note, however, that this is a completely different faith than that of the Christian. Christian faith is trusting in *The God Who Is There*. Kierkegaard's "leap of faith" is faith in faith—faith in yourself, actually. You are the creative source of life, you create the faith to bridge the gap, and you create your own meaning and purpose in the upper story. These ideas are the foundations of postmodernism.

Both Eastern mysticism and Western postmodernism have followed Plato—there must be something more than what is seen. We are now in the early years of postmodernism. As the years go by, many will find it is just as absurd to try to create your own upper story as it is to try to live only in the lower story. This is the predicament of both modern and postmodern humanity. To quote Schaeffer again:

> Modern man is left either downstairs as a machine with words that do not lead either to values or facts but only to words *(modernism)*, or he is left upstairs in a world without categories in regard to human values, moral values, or the difference between reality and fantasy *(postmodernism)*. Weep for our generation![11]

Both modernism and postmodernism are fragmented cultures. In neither is there a satisfactory way to hold the upper story and the lower story, the spiritual and the material, together. The result is despair. And despair that is not resolved turns to anger, which is directed either inward in depression or outward in violence. This is the world in which we live today—a world of rising anger. Wouldn't it be good news if there were a genuine solution to this fragmentation and the resultant anger? There is—the gap has been bridged and there is the real possibility of an integrated life!

Integration
We have already looked at the ways in which God has revealed himself to us. Not surprisingly, these also embody the three ways the gap between the spiritual realm and the material realm has been and continues to be bridged. First, it was bridged in creation. "God is spirit" (Jn. 4:24), yet he created this material world as a home for the human race that he created "in his own image" (Gen. 1:27). As the old song says, "This is my Father's world." He entrusted it to the human race and told them to "take care of it" (Gen. 2:15). The Bible is not into the dualism of other religions that see the spiritual realm as good and the material world as evil. God created it *all* good. The fact that we humans exercised our God-given free will to mess it up does not change this.

Second, God again bridged the gap in the person of Jesus, to bring redemption to this fallen world:

> In the beginning was the Word, and the Word was with God, and the Word was God....The Word became flesh and made his dwelling among us. We have seen his glory, the glory of the One and Only, who came from the Father, full of grace and truth. (Jn. 1:1,14)

Third, when Jesus completed his mission and returned to his Father, he sent the Holy Spirit to be the presence of the Living God in the world today, as we have already seen. Through the Holy Spirit, the gap continues to be bridged. The culture of the kingdom is an integrated rather than a fragmented culture. It has integrity.

Paul's understanding of this is evident in his words to the Colossians concerning Jesus:

> He is the image of the invisible God, the firstborn over all creation. For by him all things were created: things in heaven and on earth, visible and invisible, whether thrones or powers or rulers or authorities; all things were created by him and for him. He is before all things, and *in him all things hold together* (1:15-17, emphasis added)

All things hold together! Isn't that *genuine* good news? It is because of this reality that I speak of a spiritual world and a material world, rather than a natural one and a supernatural one. If we think of natural as opposed to artificial, then both God *and* his creation are *natural*, and any culture that leaves God out of the picture becomes an *artificial* culture—a manmade one, unnatural and a poor substitute for what God intended.

The End Result of Artificial Cultures

Because God created this earth and created us in his image, any culture that refuses to recognize and give proper place to God becomes an artificial culture—a fragmented culture that simply won't hold together. This is not a trivial thing. Paul spelled out the end result of an artificial culture:

> What happened was this: People knew God perfectly well, but when they didn't treat him like God, refusing to worship him, they trivialized themselves into silliness and confusion so that there was neither sense nor direction left in their lives. They pretended to know it all, but were illiterate regarding life. They traded the glory of God who holds the whole world in his hands for cheap figurines you can buy at any roadside stand.
> So God said, in effect, "If that's what you want, that's what you get." It wasn't long before they were living in a pigpen, smeared with filth, filthy inside and out. And all this because they traded the true God for a fake god, and worshiped the god they made instead of the God who made them—the God we bless, the God who blesses us. Oh, yes! (Rom. 1:21-25, *The Message*).

The reason for this should be evident to us, as it was to Plato—unless there is something absolute, morals do not exist. Without a moral God there is no moral code. Without a moral code, there is no basis for morality. Without a basis for morality, there is no moral discernment. People end up with "neither sense nor direction left in their lives."

But that's not the only fallout from ignoring God. God is the author of life (Acts 3:15), and he put humankind into a class of life by itself—created in the image of God (Gen. 1:26). Because of this, it is impossible to continue to have a proper respect for human life apart from a proper respect for God. Animal rights activists of our day think they are elevating animal life to the same level as human life—but they are not. They are lowering human life to the same level as animal life. As Ravi Zacharias notes, "The farther we move from God, the more we devalue man."[12]

In spite of Paul's admonition, Rome refused to recognize God and Roman culture became an artificial culture. It ended up destroying itself from the inside out. The lack of moral discernment and loss of respect for human life led to 50,000 screaming Romans in the Colosseum—including the Emperor in his special ring-side seat—cheering as people were torn to bits by lions. One of the most moving moments of my life came as I stood in the ruins of the Colosseum, closed my eyes, and envisioned the Christians being thrown to the lions in front of that cheering and cursing throng. Is that a genuine culture—or a sorry imitation of the real thing?

Paul's words addressed to the Romans and the fate of Roman culture should be very sobering to us today. We also live in a culture that is making less and less room for God. Consequently, like Rome more than fifteen centuries ago, our culture becomes more and more artificial—less like what God intended for us.

Could our culture degenerate to this same level of depravity as did the Roman? As people lose moral discernment and respect for human life, and as the level of anger rises, the depth to which this can reach is almost unbelievable. As an adoptive parent of two brain-damaged, abused children, I live with the evidence of this reality every day.

I also read about it regularly. As I write this, within the last month, the step-mother of a four-year-old girl in my home state taped the little girl's wrists together and her mouth shut with duct tape and then proceeded to beat her to death with a broken cutting board while the girl's father stood by. And this was not an isolated incident of uncontrollable rage—the 911 call that brought sheriff's deputies to the home to discover the little child's battered and lifeless body was the 44th visit of deputies to the home over a five-year period.[13]

In spite of what many people want to believe, we are living in an artificial, deteriorating culture—whether modern or postmodern. The rising tide of anger is one of the clearest indications of this. Is there a solution? Is there any *genuine* good news—good news that can actually transform lives?

The Genuine Good News for an Artificial Culture
The answer is...Yes! There *is* good news—a genuine gospel for an artificial world. Jesus came claiming this to be true. He proclaimed a genuine, alternative culture, the "kingdom of God," real and present on this earth—a culture in which "all things hold together." And he declared this to be good news! Reading through the New Testament will confirm this without question. Furthermore, this good news he brought was so central to what Jesus was about, that the four accounts of his life and ministry in the New Testament are called "Gospels"—a word meaning "good news."

But what *was* the good news that Jesus brought? Unfortunately, not everything that's called the *gospel* today really is. Just as there are artificial cultures, there are artificial gospels—manmade versions of the genuine one. In the next chapter we will look first at some of these popular, yet artificial gospels proclaimed today, and then examine the genuine version proclaimed by Jesus and the New Testament church. Artificial gospels lack the power of God to transform lives and establish an authentic kingdom culture in our world today—"having a form of godliness but denying its power" (2 Tim. 3:5). The gospel proclaimed by Jesus is the good news that transforms!

An Invitation
I invite you to join me in a brief journey through the remaining pages of this book. Who knows? Like millions of others, you may decide to commit to a lifelong journey with Jesus. Ordinary folks from every walk of life in every century since Jesus have considered the man and his message—and have

found in him good news for everyday life and for all eternity! Their transformed and integrated lives are perhaps the most compelling evidence yet for the reality of the God they serve.

And, not only have they found meaning and purpose in life; they have found that a living relationship with God results in a life that holds together—one that can meet the other five needs that Gallup identified, as well. To me, that beats a "free 42-inch Plasma TV" any day of the week!

Chapter 2

What Is the Good News?

> I am astonished that you are so quickly deserting the one who called you by the grace of Christ and are turning to a different gospel—which is really no gospel at all. (Galatians 1:6-7)

> It is hardly a wonder that the country that gave the world instant tea and instant coffee should be the one to give it instant Christianity. (A. W. Tozer[1])

Sometimes simple is good. Sometimes it is simply incomplete. Sometimes it is downright tragic—because it causes us to miss the heart of something true. All of these things can be said about different versions of the good news of Jesus that have developed over the years.

The good news of Jesus *is* simple, in that it is not too difficult for ordinary people to understand. What the Bible says about God's law can also be said about the gospel:

> Now what I am commanding you today is not too difficult for you or beyond your reach...No, the word is

very near you; it is in your mouth and in your heart so you may obey it. (Deut. 30:11, 14)

The gospel is simple enough for ordinary people to grasp. However, it can also be over-simplified to the point where it actually becomes a "different gospel—which is really no gospel at all," as Paul wrote. When this happens, we have an artificial gospel—an imitation of the genuine one.

Artificial Gospels

As we saw in the last chapter, people who reject or ignore God create artificial cultures. This does not mean that everything about those cultures is false. It simply means that, when compared to the wholeness of the kingdom of God, they are a poor and limited imitation of the real thing. At the center of the kingdom of God is Jesus as King of Kings and Lord of Lords, and "in him all things hold together" (Col. 1:17). Without him, there is no wholeness—things do *not* hold together. The culture becomes fragmented.

The same principle holds true when people espouse a gospel different than did Jesus or Paul: they create artificial gospels. Again, this does not mean everything about them is false. It means they are poor and limited imitations that lack the transforming power of the genuine one.

There is a reciprocating relationship between artificial cultures and artificial gospels. Artificial gospels are often created when the dominant artificial culture gains influence and subtly changes the values practiced by the church. The beliefs often stay the same but the values change. If I want to know what someone believes, I will *ask* them. But if I want to know what they value, I will *watch* them, for we live out our values. This divide between beliefs and values is a major problem in the church today and is behind much of the fragmentation we see in the lives of Christians.

The resulting artificial gospel then, in turn, undergirds the artificial culture that birthed it by providing what seems to be religious legitimacy. For example, a materialistic culture seduces the church and the church, in turn, develops a *prosperity gospel* that says this is how God designed it. The problem is, both culture and gospel are artificial, and there is no transforming power released to restore the culture to a kingdom culture.

The problem with all artificial gospels is that they are fundamentally unbalanced. They major in certain scriptures while ignoring others that are equally important. Consequently, they end up with the same problem as the artificial cultures they are trying to reach—they fail to keep the upper story and lower story of life integrated. Some are overbalanced in the direction of the spiritual realm and lose an appropriate connection to real, everyday physical existence. Others are overbalanced in the direction of the material world and fail to value the real God and the spiritual realm.

The apostle Paul used strong language when referring to those who present a different gospel. He considered this so serious that he wrote, "If anybody is preaching to you a gospel other than what you accepted, let him be eternally condemned!" (Gal. 1:8). As we have already seen, the word "gospel" means "good news." A "different gospel" is *no* gospel because it is *not* good news at all—it neither transforms our lives now nor does it guarantee our future. This is serious business!

What are some of the artificial gospels around today? We will look at four of the more prevalent ones in today's world.

The "Try Harder" Gospel

The *try harder* gospel gives special attention to scripture passages such as "Do not let sin reign in your mortal body so that you obey its evil desires" (Rom. 6:12), but ignores "For it is by grace you have been saved, through faith—and this not from yourselves, it is the gift of God—not by works, so that no one can boast" (Eph. 2:8-9). It is all about what we do. People who fall for this artificial gospel know that what we do with our lives is important. They know there is truth and that truth is to be lived out. The problem is they think they can and must do this on their own: "I can do it if I just try harder." Ultimately, it's a matter of pride; we don't like to be dependent upon others, even upon God.

This gospel is unbalanced in the direction of the lower story, in that everything depends upon us and our actions. It does not adequately understand how God has bridged the gap and entered into our world to empower us to obey him.

Typically, people who embrace the *try harder* gospel find no peace in life. They spend their lives trying to be religious and please God—to do enough to make him happy, so that when they die God will let them into heaven. Often they have spent their childhood trying to please a parent that simply will not be pleased. This gospel can also be called a *works* gospel: it's our good works that earn our way into heaven—and hopefully we've done enough. The problem is, how much *is* enough?

That was a problem that daily haunted the reformer Martin Luther (1483-1546) until he had a genuine encounter with God. As a monk, his life was spent trying to please God and save himself. Life was filled with such things as fasting, vigils, and mortification of the flesh. He went beyond the rules of the monastery and did such things as holding a vigil in a freezing cold room with no blankets. In 1510, he journeyed to Rome and walked up the steps of St. Peter's on his hands and knees, kissing each step and repeating the "Our Father" prayer with each step, as well. When he got to the top he stood up and said, "Who knows whether it is so?"

Then one day while studying Romans 1:17, he had an encounter with God that changed his life. In his own words:

> Night and day I pondered until I saw the connection between the justice of God and the statement that "the just shall live by his faith." Then I grasped that the justice of God is that righteousness by which through grace and sheer mercy God justifies us through faith. Thereupon I felt myself to be reborn and to have gone through open doors into paradise. The whole of Scripture took on a new meaning, and whereas before the "justice of God" had filled me with hate, now it became to me inexpressibly sweet in greater love. This passage of Paul became to me a gate to heaven.[2]

People who embrace the *try harder* gospel often end up being some of the most religious people around—and the most miserable. They need to encounter God and his truth in the same way that Martin Luther did to find the freedom and joy that he found.

The "Just Believe" Gospel

Most roads have a ditch on either side. If the *try harder* gospel is the ditch on one side, then the *just believe gospel* is the ditch on the other. This gospel lifts up "Believe in the Lord Jesus, and you will be saved" (Acts 16:31). It embraces Ephesians 2:8,9 mentioned above, but fails to go on to verse 10: "For we are God's workmanship, created in Christ Jesus to do good works, which God prepared in advance for us to do." We will look at this more in depth in Chapter Four.

In this *just believe* gospel it doesn't matter what we do, only what we believe. The gospel gets simply reduced to "Jesus died for your sins." All we need to do is believe that. As Dallas Willard has pointed out, when this version of the gospel is presented, it often reduces people's understanding of the gospel to two events—the first when they prayed the sinner's prayer and the second when they die and go to heaven.[3]

It is certainly true that Jesus died to provide forgiveness of our sins. And, it is indeed good news that we have a home in heaven when we leave this earthly life. However, this oversimplification of the gospel is lopsided: it does not address at all how the good news of Jesus connects to our lives *between* these two points—how it is good news for everyday living. For people who buy into the *just believe* gospel, Christianity is about praying the sinner's prayer, perhaps experiencing a great worship experience once a week—and then living just like their neighbors the rest of the week. Discipleship is a nice idea if you have time for it, but who really does with all that's involved in the great American lifestyle?

This *just believe gospel* produces the "instant Christianity" that A.W. Tozer referred to at the beginning of this chapter:

Instant Christianity came in with the machine age. Men invented machines for two purposes. They wanted to get important work done more quickly and easily than they ever could do by hand, and they wanted to get the work over with so they could give their time to pursuits more to their liking, such as loafing or enjoying the pleasures of the world. Instant Christianity now serves the same purposes in religion. It disposes of the past, guarantees the future and sets the Christian free to follow the more refined lusts of the flesh in all good conscience and with a minimum of restraint.[4]

This kind of oversimplification can also be tragic: it can give people a false sense of security:

> Not everyone who says to me, 'Lord, Lord,' will enter the kingdom of heaven, but only he who does the will of my Father who is in heaven. Many will say to me on that day, 'Lord, Lord, did we not prophesy in your name, and in your name drive out demons and perform many miracles?' Then I will tell them plainly, 'I never knew you. Away from me, you evildoers!' (Matt. 7:21-23).

The *just believe* gospel originated out of confusion in the Western world over the meaning of the word "believe." The Hebrew culture of the Bible is a concrete culture, with a concrete language. To a Hebrew, to believe in someone is to have faith in them, to entrust your life to them, to follow them. In fact, the word normally translated as "believe" in the New Testament is also translated as "entrust" on several occasions. What it means Biblically to have faith would be another example. In the language of the Bible, to have faith is to be faithful. If you check a concordance of the Old Testament, for example, you will find that the word "faith" appears very few times in our English translations. Usually it is translated as "faithful." Even where it is translated as "faith," the context makes clear the meaning is to be faithful. Usually it is about "keeping faith" or "breaking faith," meaning to be faithful or unfaithful.

Although the original language of the New Testament was Greek, the culture was largely Hebrew. Now we come to this New Testament out of our Western culture and mindset, derived from the Greek culture. We think abstractly. To believe in God is to believe abstractly and intellectually that he exists, not to trust him and follow him. But even the New Testament itself addresses this problem:

> What good is it, my brothers, if a man claims to have faith but has no deeds? Can such faith save him? Suppose a brother or sister is without clothes and daily food. If one of you says to him, "Go, I wish you well; keep warm and well fed," but does nothing about his physical needs, what good is it? In the same way, faith by itself, if it is not accompanied by action, is dead.
> But someone will say, "You have faith; I have deeds."
> Show me your faith without deeds, and I will show you my faith by what I do. You believe that there is one God. Good! Even the demons believe that—and shudder. (Jas. 2:14-19)

The *just believe* gospel has developed into a current version of what was called Gnosticism in New Testament times. The word comes from the Greek word for knowledge, *gnosis*. The Gnostics believed in a true God who preceded creation and who, at some point in time, split into a plurality of gods. This plurality then emanated or came forth into everything, including the human race. Within every human is now a "divine spark," or "inner man," that awaits an awakening produced neither by faith nor by works, but by the secret knowledge of all this. Salvation, then, is not from sin by way of atonement, as in Christianity. Instead, it is a rescue from ignorance through "knowledge."

The Gnostics saw creation and fall as the same. The god who created things (the Demiurge) was a flawed expression of the true god, and so the creation itself was flawed. They saw Yahweh, the God of Israel, as this flawed expression of God, and saw the moral law of the Old Testament in a very negative light. Therefore, they were actually encouraged to rebel against this moral law.

By contrast, they saw Jesus not as the Son of God (Yahweh) but as a good "Messenger of Light" coming forth from the good and true God that existed before creation. They accepted some of the teachings of Jesus but saw no connection between Jesus and Yahweh, Israel's God.

What was important to them was their personal experience of the knowledge of the divine inner spark. Because they saw the moral code as a flawed expression of a flawed god, their conduct was guided totally by their inner experience rather than any behavioral code. They were free to live according to their inner experience, wherever that might take them.

For some, this led to an extreme asceticism, as they saw the flawed creation as evil, including their own bodies. A second type of Gnostic living was more widespread. In this type, since creation and the moral code were the flawed work of the Demiurge, they were free from any moral constraints on their behavior, which resulted in much loose living.

The widespread existence of this *just believe* gospel, this present-day Gnosticism, has been recognized both inside and outside the church. Inside, the research of both George Gallup Jr. and George Barna have documented the disconnect between peoples' beliefs and their behaviors. Outside, Harold Bloom writes in *The American Religion*:

> We think we are Christian, but we are not. The issue is not religion in America but rather what I call the American Religion. ... There are indeed millions of Christians in the United States, but most Ameri-

cans who think that they are Christians truly are something else, intensely religious but devout in the American Religion, a faith that is old among us, and that comes in many guises and disguises.[5]

Ancient Gnosticism was an elite religion, or quasi-religion; the oddity of our American Gnosis is that it is a mass phenomenon. There are tens of millions of Americans whose obsessive idea of spiritual freedom violates the normative basis of historical Christianity, though they are incapable of realizing how little they share of what once was considered Christian doctrine.[6]

This *just believe* gospel is an upper story gospel in which one's own subjective experience of spiritual knowledge is all that actually matters. The tragedy is that it leaves everyday life in the lower story, the real physical world, unchanged from the mess that it wallows in. Thus, there is no genuine transformation and we are left to live out life in a fragmented and artificial culture. This artificial gospel has little if anything of value to offer the artificial cultures in which we live, whether modern or postmodern, and has consequently become irrelevant to them.

The "Create Your Own" Gospel

The *create your own* gospel doesn't actually lift up any particular scripture—because the scriptures aren't very important to this gospel. Retired Episcopalian Bishop John Spong, perhaps the chief proponent of this variation on the good news writes, "There is no external, objective, revealed standard writ in scripture or on tablets of stone that will govern our ethical behavior for all time."[7]

Because there are no standards "for all time," what is important is being culturally relevant—which means embracing the current culture. This *create your own* gospel is very much an upper story, postmodern gospel. Since there is no real, "for all time" God in the upper story, you must create your own culturally relevant god and theological ideas that go with it. George Gallup, Jr. and Timothy Jones give a classic illustration of this as they quote an earlier writer who described her faith like this: "Mine was a patchwork God, sewn together from bits of rag and ribbon, Eastern and Western, pagan and Hebrew, everything but the kitchen sink and Jesus thrown in."[8]

Proponents of this gospel may use a lot of the same language that other Christians do, but who knows what they really mean? For example, when Bishop Spong writes, "Resurrection is an action of God. Jesus was raised into the meaning of God,"[9] what does he mean? Since it is clear that he does not believe in a literal, historical resurrection, it's clear that these words mean something different to him than they do to Biblical Christians. But in postmodern thinking, it should not even be important to me what this means to *him*, only what it means to *me*. This is the deconstructionist method of interpretation that is very much at the heart of postmodernism. It makes genuine communication next to impossible—another cause of the rising level of anger mentioned in the previous chapter.

Bishop Spong, and others like him, are ready to completely redefine Christianity according to the current postmodern culture. And once you do away with a real God and any objective standards, who has a better idea? This redefinition goes to the very core of what Christianity is about. Again, to quote Bishop Spong: "The view of the cross as the sacrifice for the sins of the world is a barbarian idea based on primitive concepts of God and must be dismissed."[10]

Alan Wolfe, another outside observer, has noted this kind of redefinition in his book *The Transformation of American Culture: How We Actually Live Our Faith:*

H. Richard Niebuhr documented the many ways in which Christ could become a transformer of culture. But in the United States culture has transformed Christ, as well as all other religions found within these shores. In every aspect of the religious life, American faith has met American culture—and American culture has triumphed...

The message of this book is that religion in the United States is being transformed in radically new directions.[11]

Bishop Spong and others believe this is the only way to "save" Christianity, to get people back to the church who have checked out. And, judging from the CBS "60 Minutes" interview with Bishop Spong which aired May 21, 2000, some people are certainly doing this. But if it no longer bears even a faint resemblance to Biblical Christianity, what are they coming back to? Being culturally relevant is *not* just embracing all the ideas and assumptions of the dominant culture. It *is* caring enough about it to understand it and to offer it something genuine as an alternative.

"American faith has met American culture—and American culture has triumphed." An artificial culture has created an artificial gospel. The transformation here is in the wrong direction. It will reveal not the glory of God but, ultimately, the "silliness and confusion" of postmodern humanity, resulting in "neither sense nor direction left in their lives" (Rom. 1:22, *The Message*). I can only say with Schaeffer, "Weep for our generation!"

The "Role Reversal" Gospel

The *role reversal* gospel is another result of the human-centered culture—whether the modern or postmodern version—

that dominates the present day. Because we have become conditioned to seeing ourselves as the center of the universe, we are now the masters and God is the servant.

In the early years of my pastoral ministry, I worked with a young man named Danny. Danny had attended the youth group at our church before I came there as pastor, but had dropped out at some point. Soon after I came, he started coming to church occasionally and we developed a friendship that has continued to this day—but not without its rocky moments!

Danny had struggled for years with a cross-addiction to alcohol and other drugs. This continued to be a struggle for him, even after he made his first commitment to Jesus as his Savior. As our friendship grew, I noticed a very clear pattern of behavior. When life seemed to be under control and things were going well, I would see very little of him. Then, when he got back into the alcohol and drugs and things fell apart, he would be back.

At one of those points, he came back around again, upset at God and just about everyone else because his life wasn't working well. It happened to be a day when I wasn't ready to go back around the same mountain again. I looked at Danny and said, "You know what, man? You think God is your errand boy. When things are going well, you don't give him the time of day, and when they aren't, you want to be able to snap your fingers and he is supposed to jump to your service and straighten out your life again. I want to tell you something: He isn't your errand boy; He is God!"

This upset Danny and I didn't see him again for two or three months. Then one day my phone rang:

"Hey, this is Dan. Do you remember what you told me?"
"I've told you a lot of things! What are you referring to?"
"About me thinking that God was my errand boy?"

"Yes, I remember that," I responded. "What about it?"

"Well, I've been thinking about that, and I have come to the conclusion that you were right. I have been treating God as though he were my errand boy!"

Danny had gotten hold of the *role reversal* gospel. He did what he wanted with his life. He called the shots, and it was God's job to make sure that things worked the way he wanted them to work. He was the master and God was the servant. Only a new encounter with the Living God and his truth could put things back in order: where God is Master and Lord, and we are his servants.

We prayed together and Danny confessed this as sin. Danny had a new encounter with the Living God that was the beginning of a new season in his life. Not everything has been rosy since, but today he is drug and alcohol free and is actually in training to be in full-time ministry as I write this.

There is a variation of the *role reversal* gospel that could well be called the *magic* gospel. In this version, you can use the words God has spoken to manipulate him into doing what you want. You want a new silver-colored Lexus? You need to believe that God wants to bless you and that "whatever you ask for in prayer, believe that you have received it, and it will be yours" (Mk. 11:24). After all, this is the Word of God and God has to honor his word!

It is true that God loves us, and wants to bless us—and that he has invited us to petition him for "our daily bread," the things that we need for the fulfilled life he desires for us. But it's also true that the motive behind our asking makes all the difference: "You do not have, because you do not ask God. When you ask, you do not receive, because you ask with wrong motives, that you may spend what you get on your pleasures" (Jas. 4:2,3).

The *prosperity* gospel is another variation of the *role reversal* gospel: the idea that God wants you to be rich. Within the last year, I sat in a service and listened as a preacher whipped the crowd into an emotional frenzy with a message that could well be summed up as "God wants you to have the gold!" Not once in that message did I hear anything about the claim of God on our lives, only about our claim on his gold! I went home greatly grieved over what I had heard and observed. The man forgot the words of Paul about "men of corrupt mind, who have been robbed of the truth and who think that godliness is a means to financial gain" (1 Tim. 6:5). Paul had a different message:

> But godliness with contentment is great gain. For we brought nothing into the world, and we can take nothing out of it. But if we have food and clothing, we will be content with that. People who want to get rich fall into temptation and a trap and into many foolish and harmful desires that plunge men into ruin and destruction. For the love of money is a root of all kinds of evil. Some people, eager for money, have wandered from the faith and pierced themselves with many griefs.
>
> But you, man of God, flee from all this, and pursue righteousness, godliness, faith, love, endurance and gentleness. (1 Tim. 6:6-11).

The *role reversal* gospel is another example of the reciprocating action between artificial culture and artificial gospel. Postmodern culture with its "create your own upper story" ideas has led to Christians uncritically accepting these same ideas. Now we have developed an artificial gospel that says with postmodern culture, "You can be whatever you want to be."

This is actually a pagan rather than a Christian idea: *if you could be whatever you wanted to be, you would be God.* It's interesting that pagans themselves fully recognize this to be a pagan idea. There was a pagan alliance in our area some time ago whose logo on their website read, "Our fate is ours to create." I often wonder why so many Christians repeat this same thing without once thinking about what they are actually saying.

The *role reversal* gospel is the result of preaching the truth that God desires to bless us and meet our needs, but preaching it *out of season* to people who have learned little or nothing about serving God: "There is a time for everything, and a season for every activity under heaven" (Eccl. 3:1). This is a season to set the roles straight. As has been said many times over the years and again recently in a popular song, "God is God and we are not!" As a friend once said to me, "Being God is a big job! If you try it, it will probably kill you!"

If a self-centered and self-focused, yet artificial and fragmented culture is to be transformed by the power of God, people must hear and submit to this truth. It's only as we place ourselves in service to God's Kingdom that we find life to be integrated and truly fulfilling, as we shall see.

The Genuine Gospel

Thankfully, in the midst of all the artificial gospels of our time, there is a real one! This is not a time to wring our hands, but a time to rediscover the genuine gospel for an artificial world. To do so, we must lay aside the preconceived ideas that we have and return to the New Testament—to look afresh at the gospel that was proclaimed by Jesus and by the New Testament church—the gospel that really is good news for all of life!

The Good News Proclaimed by Jesus

As we have already seen in the previous chapter, at the very beginning of his ministry Jesus proclaimed, "The time has

WHAT IS THE GOOD NEWS?

come...the kingdom of God is near. Repent and believe the good news!" (Mk. 1:15). This "gospel of the kingdom" was to be central throughout his ministry.

Early in his ministry, Jesus stopped in the town of Capernaum. Sick people were brought to Jesus and they were healed. People under demonic influence were set free. The people of Capernaum were so thrilled with this good news proclaimed and demonstrated by Jesus that they tried to talk him into staying with them. But Jesus was so focused on his mission that he was able to resist the pressure to stay: "I must preach the good news of the kingdom of God to the other towns also, because that is why I was sent" (Lu. 4:43).

Somewhat later, in Luke 8:1, we read, "After this, Jesus traveled about from one town and village to another, proclaiming the good news of the kingdom of God." On one occasion as he was speaking about John the Baptist, he said, "The Law and the Prophets were proclaimed until John. Since that time, the good news of the kingdom of God is being preached, and everyone is forcing his way into it" (Lu. 16:16).

When instructing his disciples how to pray, he gave them a pattern prayer:

> Our Father in heaven, hallowed be your name, *your kingdom come, your will be done on earth as it is in heaven.* Give us today our daily bread. Forgive us our debts, as we also have forgiven our debtors. And lead us not into temptation, but deliver us from the evil one. (Matt. 6:9-13, emphasis added).

Even as Jesus' years of ministry drew to a close, just prior to his death on the cross, it was this message of the kingdom of God that was on his lips. As he ate the Last Supper with his disciples he said, "I have eagerly desired to eat this Passover with you before I suffer. For I tell you, I will not eat it again until it finds fulfillment in the kingdom of God" (Lu. 22:15,16).

Then, after his death and resurrection, he shared his last 40 days on earth with these men closest to him "and spoke about the kingdom of God" (Acts 1:3). From the beginning to the end of his earthly ministry, Jesus stayed focused on this message that he called "the good news of the kingdom."

The Good News Proclaimed by the Church
But what about the church that was left behind when Jesus returned to heaven? What did they proclaim as the "good news?" Did they simply proclaim "Jesus died for your sins?" Or, did they proclaim the same message Jesus proclaimed—but with an added dimension now?

In Acts 8:12, we read that Phillip "preached the things concerning the kingdom of God and the name of Jesus Christ." Likewise, as we come to the end of the book of Acts, we find Paul a prisoner in a house in Rome, yet free to welcome those who came to him. There, "Boldly and without hindrance he preached the kingdom of God and taught about the Lord Jesus Christ" (Acts 28:31). In other words, both Phillip and Paul taught the same thing that Jesus had taught about the kingdom of God, and now added to this message the role that Jesus' life, death, and resurrection played in this good news.

This message of the kingdom was proclaimed by virtually every New Testament writer. James wrote, "Has not God chosen those who are poor in the eyes of the world to be rich in faith and to inherit the kingdom he promised those who love him?" (Jas. 2:5). Peter wrote that those who remain faithful "will receive a rich welcome into the eternal kingdom of our Lord and Savior Jesus Christ" (2 Pet. 1:10). The writer of the letter to the Hebrews, who is not identified, wrote that "since we are receiving a kingdom that cannot be shaken, let us be thankful, and so worship God acceptably with reverence and awe" (Heb. 12:28). And in the Revelation, as John wrote of the vision he had seen, he reported there were loud voices in heaven proclaiming, "The kingdom of the world has become the kingdom of our Lord and of his Christ, and he will reign for ever and ever."

Thus, from the beginning of Jesus' ministry through the end of New Testament church history, this "good news of the kingdom" was central to the message. Indeed, it was Jesus' clear intent that it would be central as long as this earth remains: "This gospel of the kingdom will be preached in the whole world as a testimony to all nations, and then the end will come" (Matt. 24:14).

But What Does It Mean?

We have little understanding of "kingdoms" today. If we hear of "kingdoms" at all in the English-speaking regions of this 21st century world in which we live, it usually has to do with the royal family in the United Kingdom—who are involved in a lot of pomp and circumstance but have very little if anything to do with actual government. That is handled by the Parliament and government ministers.

As a result, there is also little understanding of what Jesus was actually talking about when he spoke about the "good news of the kingdom of God." Before we can understand the *good news* of the kingdom, we must first back up and answer the question, *"What is the kingdom of God?"* There is simply no way to comprehend what Jesus was about without first considering this matter. In the next chapter we will answer this foundational question, and then move on to define the good news of the kingdom in Chapter Four. As we do, we will find it is not the "instant Christianity" that Tozer referred to—but neither is it too difficult to understand, if we will only take sufficient time out from our a·muse·ment to muse a bit.

Chapter 3

The Kingdom of God

> In the beginning God created the heavens and the earth. The earth was empty, a formless mass cloaked in darkness. And the Spirit of God was hovering over its surface. Then God said, "Let there be light," and there was light. (Genesis 1:1-3, NLT)

As we discussed in the previous chapter, the word "kingdom" is one little used and little understood in our Western world. Yet, if we are to understand the message of the Bible and the mission of Jesus, we must understand kingdom language.

A kingdom can be simply defined as *a sphere of influence in which a king rules.* Within his kingdom, whatever the king says, goes. In the beginning, God spoke this world into existence. What he said, happened. When he said, "Let there be light," light burst forth where everything had been "cloaked in darkness."

By virtue of the fact that God created this earth, the earth was his kingdom and he was the king. "I am the LORD, your Holy One, Israel's Creator, your King" (Isa. 43:15). And he had a plan to involve us in his kingdom! While that opened up some exciting opportunities for us, it also led to a problem for all of creation! We will see this as we endeavor to understand two kingdoms—the kingdom of God and the kingdom of this world.

Understanding Two Kingdoms

The diagram below consists simply of seven lines, two horizontal and five vertical.[1] Yet, if we understand the realities represented by these lines, we will have a good framework for

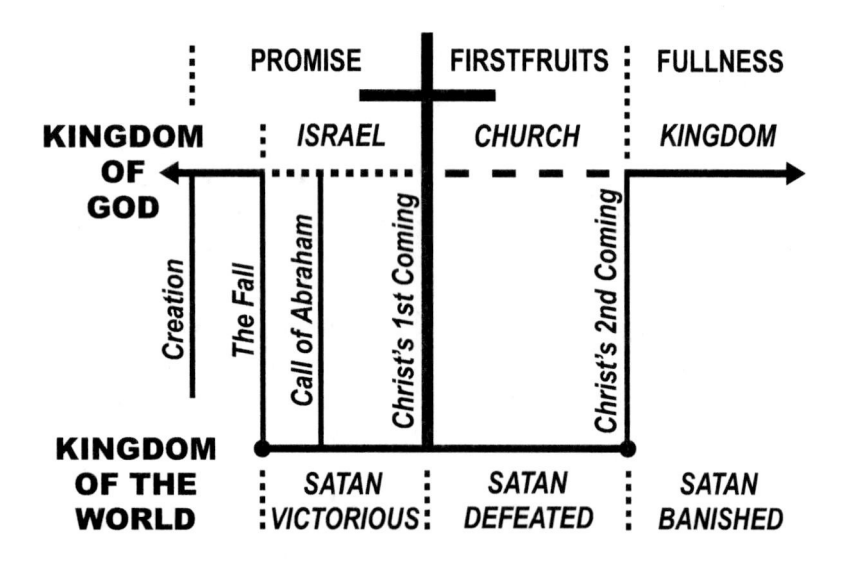

```
                    PROMISE      FIRSTFRUITS    FULLNESS
KINGDOM             ISRAEL         CHURCH       KINGDOM
OF GOD

           Creation  The Fall  Call of Abraham  Christ's 1st Coming  Christ's 2nd Coming

KINGDOM
OF THE              SATAN          SATAN         SATAN
WORLD             VICTORIOUS      DEFEATED      BANISHED
```

understanding the whole of Scripture. Virtually all of Scripture can be hung on this skeleton to get the big picture of the Bible. Many heresies have come into the church because people have rushed to particular passages of Scripture without first taking the time to get the big picture. And as we get the big picture we will find that central to it is the kingdom of God.

The two horizontal lines represent the kingdom of God and "the kingdom of the world" (Rev. 11:15). The top line represents the kingdom of God and has arrows on both ends, representing a kingdom with neither beginning nor end: "Your kingdom is an everlasting kingdom, and your dominion endures through all generations" (Ps. 145:13). The second line has a definite beginning and end, as does the kingdom of this world. The "kingdom of the world" of Revelation 11:15 is made up of all the "kingdoms of the world" (Matthew 4:8). All the artificial cultures of humankind are included in this bottom line.

The five vertical lines represent five key historical events, four that have already happened and one yet to come. Let's look now at each of these vertical lines and see what they tell us about the two horizontal ones.

Creation

As we have already seen, God first bridged the gap between the upper story and the lower story—the spiritual realm and the physical realm—in creation. "God is spirit" (Jn. 4:24) and he created the physical universe that now stands as a general revelation of the character and purpose of God.

In the first two chapters of the Bible, we have two complementary pictures of this creation. In the first, which covers all of creation, we see the all-powerful God who simply spoke forth his will and this world came into existence. In the second, focused on the human race as the crown of this creation, we see an all-loving God intimately involved with these humans and their environment.

A friend of mine refers to these as pictures of the "Most High God" and the "Most Nigh God."[2] The God who says, "As the heavens are higher than the earth, so are my ways higher than your ways" (Isaiah 55:8), is *also* "a friend who sticks closer than a brother" (Prov. 18:24).

Just as people throughout history have found it difficult to keep the spiritual world and the physical world integrated into one whole, so have they found it difficult to keep these two pictures of God together and in balance. At times, they have seen only the "Most High God," one awesome and all-powerful—but too distant to be involved in the everyday affairs of the human race. At other times they have seen only the "Most Nigh God," and lost sight of his awesome majesty, having seen God only as a cosmic buddy whom they beckoned to do their bidding. Both are distortions of reality. Only as we hold these two pictures together do we have a healthy understanding of *The God Who Is There*.

A Fourfold Harmony of Relationships
In these two chapters, Adam and Eve lived fully under the reign or rule of God. Thus the life we see is a good picture of life in the kingdom of God. We see a fourfold harmony of relationships—with God, self, others, and creation.

It is clear that Adam was familiar with "the sound of the LORD God as he was walking in the garden in the cool of the day" (3:8). This is a picture of a close, intimate relationship between God and the human race he created. God saw that it was "not good for the man to be alone," and created Eve as a helper. This gave rise to the joy of close interpersonal relationships. (2:18,24). It is also clear they were at peace within themselves, as "they were naked, and they felt no shame" (2:25). They were open books with no shame and nothing to hide.

Finally, the setting into which they were placed was a garden, a beautiful place filled with vegetation and animals. This is a picture of harmony within the physical creation itself, as there was no sign of conflict between the animals nor between the animals and the human race.

This fourfold harmony of relationships is perhaps the best definition we can give for the Old Testament word *shalom*. This beautiful word is usually translated as "peace" but it means much more than that. It is a description of life lived fully in the kingdom of God, a picture of spiritual, emotional, social, and physical harmony. This is an integrated life, one that holds together—the kind of life for which we were created.

A Four-Fold Responsibility

The human race was also given a fourfold responsibility in regard to this creation (1:28; 2:15). First, we were to "fill the earth." We were created male and female to marry and establish families, filling the earth with our offspring.

Secondly, we were given the responsibility to "subdue" or develop the earth—to bring out of it the potential that God had created into it. Science has been a great tool for bringing out this potential. It's a sobering thought, however, to realize this potential can be used for good or for evil—depending upon the choices we make. We have developed the process of nuclear fission, which can produce either electrical power or weapons of mass destruction.

Third, God entrusted this good earth into our hands and said, "Rule over it!" The human race was the crown of God's creation, and God's desire was for us to partner with him in ruling over the rest of it. We will come back to this in the next chapter as we seek to understand "the good news of the kingdom."

Finally, we were charged with cultivating and caring for this earth. As we rule over this earth, we must do so remembering that we do not own it; we are stewards of it. We are to treat it with respect and take care of it.

Adam and Eve were given great freedom in how they would carry out these responsibilities, but it was not an unlimited freedom. They had to submit to the reigning authority of Yahweh God if they were to continue to experience shalom, allowing him to define good and evil (2:16,17). Only God has the capability to determine this, a fact that history has proven as the human race has so often ended up calling evil good and good evil.[3]

In our diagram, there is only the top horizontal line at this point. The total of human experience is lived in the kingdom of God. The created world and the kingdom of God are one and the same—integrated. Thus the creation accounts are important to our understanding of the kingdom of God because they give us a picture of life as God designed it, before it was torn apart by sin. As we will see below, it also gives us a picture of what life will one day be like again, and towards which things should be moving for Christians today.

The Fall

When we come to the third chapter of Genesis, two things happen: Another character enters the story, and everything falls apart! The serpent comes on the scene and begins his deceptive work:

> Now the serpent was more crafty than any of the wild animals the LORD God had made. He said to the woman, "Did God really say, 'You must not eat from any tree in the garden'?"
>
> The woman said to the serpent, "We may eat fruit from the trees in the garden, but God did say, 'You must not eat fruit from the tree that is in the middle of the garden, and you must not touch it, or you will die.'"

"You will not surely die," the serpent said to the woman. "For God knows that when you eat of it your eyes will be opened, and you will be like God, knowing good and evil."

It's interesting to note the devil's strategy here—because it hasn't changed. First, he loves to raise doubts in people's minds about what God has said: "Did God really say...." Second, he then tells an outright lie, contradicting God: "You will *not* surely die!" Finally, he tempts people to live independently of God, the Sin behind the sins, the root that bears all kind of bad fruit: "Your eyes will be opened, and *you will be like God*, knowing good and evil."

It should not be surprising that the devil would come with this line. It was the same idea that got him removed from the presence of God. While the origins of Satan are somewhat obscure, there are two passages in the Old Testament that seem to address this, one of which is found in Isaiah 14:12-15. Evidently he was one of the chief angels in the presence of God who wanted to take God's place, and rebelled against him:

> How you have fallen from heaven, O morning star, son of the dawn! You have been cast down to the earth, you who once laid low the nations!
> You said in your heart, "I will ascend to heaven; I will raise my throne above the stars of God; I will sit enthroned on the mount of assembly, I will ascend above the tops of the clouds; I will make myself like the Most High."
> But you are brought down to the grave, to the depths of the pit.

We usually think of rebellion as a violent thing. However, rebellion against God is not necessarily violent. Sometimes it is just polite disregard for the things of God. The slide into rebellion can begin very subtly, as we have already seen from Paul's words to the Romans. Regardless of how it begins, subtly or violently, the end result of rebellion against God is the same. People eventually end up in "silliness and confusion" with neither "sense nor direction left in their lives... illiterate regarding life" (Rom. 1:22, *The Message*).

People may have a lot of knowledge yet lack the moral discernment necessary for life to function well. The result is a path that will lead them farther and farther away from God, often into very degrading things. How many times have very gifted and talented people ended up in disgrace—persons who were designed by God to rule over the earth—because they were unable to properly rule even their own lives?

Discord Instead of Harmony

The results of rebellion against God were devastating. Harmony became discord—spiritually, emotionally, socially, physically. Instead of enjoying a walk in the cool of the day, Adam and Eve hid from God (3:8). Emotionally, shame entered the world and attempts to cover it up were underway (3:7). Instead of social harmony, the "blame game" started as Adam blamed Eve and Eve blamed the serpent (3:11-13). Physically, the beauty and tranquility of the garden gave way to pain, sweat, thistles, and thorns (3:16-19). The way to the Tree of Life was barred (3:23,24). There would be no easy way back. It would cost Jesus his life to once again open the way.

A World in Bondage

According to the New Testament, as a result of the Fall, the dominion given to humankind in creation ended up in the hands of "that old serpent," Satan. Part of Satan's temptation of Jesus was to take him up to a high place and show him all the kingdoms of the world; "I will give you all their authority and splendor, *for it has been given to me,* and I can give it to anyone I want to" (Lu. 4:5,6, emphasis added). That's what happened at the fall—dominion was handed over to the devil when Adam and Eve chose to listen to him rather than to God. John recognized this in his words, "We know that we are children of God, and that the whole world is under the control of the evil one" (1 Jn. 5:19).

It is at this point that the lower horizontal line begins. In the fall, there was a tearing apart. Adam and Eve were cast from the garden into the everyday toil among the thistles. Humankind had been given freedom of choice by the Creator, and they exercised that choice by turning their backs upon God, determined to live life out according to their will rather than the will of God. They moved from the kingdom of God to the kingdom of this world, to the kingdom of self, under the dominion of Satan. It wasn't—and still isn't—a good place to be.

This "tearing apart" and the alienation that came with it was the beginning of the difficulty of keeping the upper story and lower story of life together. The human race was now living in the lower story, in this physical creation that God had pronounced "very good" when he created it, in a fallen condition, experiencing alienation from God and from each other. This was also the beginning of the artificial cultures we looked at earlier. Once any culture becomes alienated from God, it becomes an artificial culture, a poor substitute for the way of life God intended.

Why Free Will?
The question is often asked at this point, "If God knew these consequences of our bad choices, why would he give us the freedom to choose to begin with? Why not create us so that we would automatically obey him?"

The answer to that question is found in God's character: "God is love" (1 Jn. 4:16). Love is at the heart of who God is. And love does not exist without an object. We don't just "love." We love someone or some thing. God created us in his image to be the object of his love. He wanted to have a meaningful, loving relationship with us.

He also understood that it is the choice to love that gives meaning to our relationships. That children have a relationship with their parents is a fact of biology. But biology alone does not give meaning to that relationship. It is the choice to express love in the relationship that gives meaning to it! As a biological parent, foster parent, adoptive parent, and grandparent I have experienced this reality many times!

Abraham and Israel

God is a redemptive God, not a vindictive one. He immediately declared he would frustrate Satan's schemes and redeem his fallen world. He promised that while Satan would bruise the heel of the woman's seed, that Seed would crush the headship of Satan (Gen. 3:14,15). That Seed would be Jesus, as we shall see.

God not only created the human race because he wanted a loving relationship with us. He has also chosen to work out his purposes in this earth *through people!* Think about that: God, who had the power to speak this world into existence, could certainly have chosen to work in other ways, but he didn't. Invariably, when God wants to accomplish something in this earth, he looks for a person.

Blessed to Be a Blessing

When he was ready to initiate his redeeming and restoring work, putting this torn and alienated world back together, he found a willing vessel named Abram. He called Abram out, promising him a blessing so that he could be a blessing to others:

> I will make you into a great nation and I will bless you; I will make your name great, and you will be a blessing.
> I will bless those who bless you, and whoever curses you I will curse; and all peoples on earth will be blessed through you. (Gen. 12:1-3).

Abram was faithful to the call and God truly made him into a great nation. God even changed his name from Abram, meaning "exalted father," to Abraham, meaning "father of many." I will never forget my first trip to Israel, especially a visit to a small Arab village near the Sea of Galilee. We formed a circle, along with the Arab children of the village and our Jewish guide, and taught them the "Father Abraham" children's song:

> Father Abraham had many sons
> Many sons had Father Abraham
> I am one of them, and so are you
> So let's just praise the Lord!

Here, Arab children (sons of Abraham through Ishmael), a Jew (a son of Abraham through Isaac), and American Christians (adopted sons and daughters of Abraham, according to Gal. 3:7) all joined hands in a circle to honor a man who simply answered the call of God and obeyed.

Later, this same call was given to Abraham's descendants, the nation of Israel, following their deliverance from slavery in Egypt:

"You yourselves have seen what I did to Egypt, and how I carried you on eagles' wings and brought you to myself. Now if you obey me fully and keep my covenant, then out of all nations you will be my treasured possession. Although the whole earth is mine, you will be for me a kingdom of priests and a holy nation." These are the words you are to speak to the Israelites." (Ex. 19:3-6).

For years, Israel lived with God as their king, with no earthly king over them. But following the deaths of Moses and Joshua, their zeal for God waned. They eventually came to live more in the kingdom of the world than in the kingdom of God: "In those days there was no king in Israel; everyone did what was right in his own eyes" (Judges 17:6, NKJV). Reaping the consequences of self-centered living, they spent more time in bondage to their neighbors than in freedom.

We Want a King Like our Neighbors!
Tiring of this bondage, their solution was to ask for a king like their neighbors had, rather than to return to the kingdom of God (1 Sam. 8:1-9). Samuel was not happy with their request, and took it to the Lord. The Lord responded: "Listen to all that the people are saying to you; *it is not you they have rejected, but they have rejected me as their king*" (1 Sam. 8:7, emphasis added). God warned them of the consequences, and then allowed them to have their king.

With few exceptions, from that point on the history of Israel was one of the kings leading the people astray, and God sending prophets to call them back to obedience (Amos 7:10-17). Their experience of the kingdom of God was an incomplete and imperfect one, represented by the dotted top line of the diagram on page 58.

A Time of Promise

But it would not always be so. The prophets also pointed forward to a new day when God would act decisively on their behalf, a day when the kingdom would come in a new way. It was a time of PROMISE:

> "This is the covenant I will make with the house of Israel after that time," declares the LORD. "I will put my law in their minds and write it on their hearts. I will be their God, and they will be my people. No longer will a man teach his neighbor, or a man his brother, saying, 'Know the LORD,' because they will all know me, from the least of them to the greatest," declares the LORD. "For I will forgive their wickedness and will remember their sins no more." (Jer. 31:31-34)

Understanding the call of Abraham is essential to understanding the kingdom of God, as it is the beginning of redemptive history. "Blessed to be a blessing" was the call to Abraham, and to all who would follow in his footsteps. This is what the kingdom of God is about, being set free from oneself to serve Christ and his kingdom, and to cooperate with God in carrying out his purposes.

Christ's First Coming—Salvation

After a long spiritual drought in Israel, the time of fulfillment came. "But when the time had fully come, God sent his Son, born of a woman, born under law, to redeem those under law, that we might receive the full rights of sons" (Gal. 4:4,5).

The Life of Jesus

Sometimes we rush too quickly over the life of Christ, finding significance only in his death and resurrection. But his life was important as well. We have already seen that he came to reveal the character and purpose of God. He also came to demonstrate what life in the kingdom of God looks like—a life in which the upper story and lower story are fully integrated.

We have already defined a kingdom as *a sphere of influence in which a king rules.* Therefore, wherever God rules we find an expression of the kingdom of God. We have also seen that the experience of Israel was a limited and incomplete expression of God's kingdom, as they walked sometimes in obedience to God, sometimes in disobedience.

With Jesus, a new expression of the kingdom was present on this earth, reflected in our diagram by the dotted line changing to a dashed line. He walked in *complete* obedience to his Father God. He came declaring, "I have come down from heaven not to do my will but to do the will of him who sent me" (John 6:38). He was so tuned in to what his Father was doing that he could say, "the Son can do nothing by himself; he can do only what he sees his Father doing, because whatever the Father does the Son also does" (John 5:19). Further, "I do nothing on my own but speak just what the Father has taught me" (Jn. 8:28). This is why he called his followers with the words, "Come, follow me!"

As he "did what he saw the Father doing," the power of God's kingdom was released in his life and ministry. When John the Baptist sat discouraged in prison, he sent some of his followers to ask of Jesus, "Are you the one who was to come, or should we expect someone else?" Jesus' reply was, "Go back and report to John what you have seen and heard: The blind receive sight, the lame walk, those who have leprosy are cured, the deaf hear, the dead are raised, and the good news is preached to the poor" (Lu. 7:20-22). He made a direct connection between the power of God and the kingdom when he was accused of casting out demons by Beelzebub, the prince of demons: "If I drive out demons by the finger of God, then the kingdom of God has come to you" (Lu. 11:20).

Whenever the power of God is released in God's kingdom, it moves people away from the brokenness and fragmentation of the artificial culture in which they live, towards the wholeness of the kingdom of God. Jesus said, "The thief comes only to steal and kill and destroy; I have come that they may have life, and have it to the full" (Jn. 10:10).

Another significant thing accomplished through the life and ministry of Jesus was the calling out of the first church, with a core group of twelve men. From among those who responded to his message, Jesus called twelve for a special role. This was not something he took lightly. Luke tells us that the night before he called the Twelve, he "went out to a mountainside to pray, and spent the night praying to God" (6:12). The next morning, he called his disciples to him and chose twelve of them, designating them apostles—meaning "ones sent out on a mission."

It was to these twelve, and especially to the inner circle of Peter, James, and John, that Jesus devoted most of the remaining time of his earthly ministry. As the twelve sons of Jacob (great grandsons of Abraham) were the founding fathers of the tribes of Old Testament Israel, so these twelve would play a similar foundational role for the New Testament Church. They would see the church established in the power of the Holy Spirit on the Day of Pentecost, after his resurrection and ascension back to heaven.

The Death and Resurrection of Jesus
While the life of Jesus was important for the reasons we have just noted, without his death and resurrection we would still be stuck in our sins and in our artificial and broken cultures. It was the atoning work of Jesus' death and resurrection that

broke the hold of Satan upon this earth and opened the doorway into the kingdom of God.

As Jesus came to the latter days of his ministry, his attention turned to Jerusalem and all that would soon happen there: "As the time approached for him to be taken up to heaven, Jesus resolutely set out for Jerusalem" (Lu. 9:51). His mission on earth could not be completed without the events of the days ahead.

As he headed toward Jerusalem, he was very clear with the disciples concerning what was about to happen:

> "We are going up to Jerusalem," he said, "and the Son of Man will be betrayed to the chief priests and teachers of the law. They will condemn him to death and will hand him over to the Gentiles, who will mock him and spit on him, flog him and kill him. Three days later he will rise." (Mk. 10:33,34)

When he arrived in Jerusalem, things went just as Jesus said they would. He was falsely accused, arrested, tried, convicted and sentenced to be crucified. As Jesus hung on the cross, I'm sure Satan thought he had won, and had eliminated the threat to his kingdom. I'm also sure that one second after the resurrection, he was aware that not only had he *not* won, he had just sealed his own fate!

> Since the children have flesh and blood, he *(Jesus)* too shared in their humanity so that by his death he might destroy him who holds the power of death—that is, the devil—and free those who all their lives were held in slavery by their fear of death. (Heb. 2:14,15)

He defeated Satan by dealing with the sin problem of the human race that had separated them from God, leading to the fragmented and artificial cultures they created. Paul sums this up well in his second letter to the Corinthian church:

> If anyone is in Christ, he is a new creation; the old has gone, the new has come! All this is from God, who reconciled us to himself through Christ and gave us the ministry of reconciliation: that God was reconciling the world to himself in Christ, not counting men's sins against them ... God made him who had no sin to be a sin offering[4] for us, so that in him we might become the righteousness of God. (2 Cor. 5:17-21)

In our world today, where being politically correct is more important than understanding truth, a lot of people have a problem with Jesus' death on the cross. Another of Bishop Spong's "twelve theses" states, "The view of the cross as the sacrifice for the sins of the world is a barbarian idea based on primitive concepts of God and must be dismissed."[5] In a CBS "60 Minutes" interview, speaking of Jesus dying for our sins, he added, "Let me tell you, I don't believe that. I think it's grotesque ... Why didn't God simply say, "I forgive you?"[6]

Why *did* Jesus need to die? Why *couldn't* God have simply said to the human race, "I forgive you?" Let's first answer this question, and then look at why Bishop Spong's view makes sense to people who embrace the ideas that are foundational to postmodern culture.

What if the stepmother who beat her four-year-old stepdaughter to death, mentioned in Chapter One, would be told by the judge she will stand before, "It's okay, I have decided to forgive you. You are free to go." What if Osama Bin Laden is never found and brought to trial for masterminding the murder of almost 3,000 people on September 11, 2001? What if there were no consequences—in this life or the life to come—for all those who have molested and murdered innocent children? What if there simply were no consequences for all the ways that people harm one another? Would you want to live in a world like that?

The thought of a world with no consequences for actions is abhorrent to anyone not totally deceived by the devil. It would be an unjust world. What does it mean to be just? It is being "Honorable and fair in one's dealings and actions... Consistent with what is morally right; righteous... Properly due or merited... Valid within the law; lawful... Suitable or proper in nature; fitting....Based on fact or sound reason; well-founded."[7]

But unless there is a real, just God who created this world and gave us his standard of what is right and just, who is to determine what is "honorable, fair, valid, suitable, or proper?" Is it whatever those in control decide? Was Hitler's murder of over six million Jews fair, valid, suitable, or proper? On what basis do we decide?

If one begins with the fundamental assumptions that lie beneath postmodern culture, then it should not be surprising that Bishop Spong and many others end up seeing absolutely no reason for Jesus to have died. Biblically, the Sin behind all sins—the root that bears bad fruit—is our desire to live independently of God, doing our own thing. A sinful attitude of rebellion against God leads to sinful actions. The predominant New Testament word for "sin" is *hamartia*, meaning "to miss the mark:" To sin is to miss the mark that God has established.

But if there were no real, just God—if the upper story is empty or contains only whatever we create there—how would we rebel against God? And if there were no standards, how would we miss the mark? And so, to those who have embraced the basic assumptions underlying postmodern culture, the idea of sin does not make sense. And if there is no sin, atonement for sin does not compute. And if there were no need of atonement, then the idea of Jesus dying on the cross for us would indeed be a grotesque idea.

But if there is a real, just and moral God who has revealed in history what is right and what is wrong, and if we have all done wrong, or missed the mark, as Romans 3:23 declares, then there must be consequences—someone must pay. That's what Jesus did for us.

One last point here: there are those who would say the idea of God requiring Jesus, an innocent man, to die for us would itself be an unjust action. And, indeed, *if* God had required Jesus to die *against his will*, he would have violated the free will God has given to every person, and it would have been an unjust action. However, that is not the case. Jesus said, "I lay down my life ... No one takes it from me, but I lay it down of my own accord" (Jn. 10:17,18).

This was and is the supreme act of love that stands as the climax in the drama of world history! What remains is the denouement—to see the final outcome of that victory over evil played out before our eyes. Better yet, we get to participate in the denouement as we fulfill the part assigned to us by God himself.

The Era of Firstfruits

With his life, death and resurrection, Jesus paid the price of sin and defeated Satan, breaking his hold on all of creation. In so doing, he opened the door to a new day in the kingdom of God, a day of FIRSTFRUITS. The kingdom of God was here in a new way, yet not in all its fullness. This is the time in which we now live. Having raised him from the dead, Acts 2:36 declares that God has now "made Jesus both Lord and Christ." Now, to recognize God as king and to live in the kingdom of God is to place our faith and trust in Jesus as Savior and Lord, by way of God's grace to us (Eph.2:8,9). Those who receive Jesus as Savior and Lord make up the church. Local churches become "outposts of the Kingdom." That phrase is not original with me, but I no longer remember where it came from, and do not know whom to credit. It is one of my favorite definitions of the church, for reasons that will become clear in the next chapter.

Those who are now "in Christ" have established their citizenship in the kingdom of God: "For he has rescued us from the dominion of darkness and brought us into the kingdom of the Son he loves" (Col. 1:13). We now have a whole new set of possibilities before us. We have a new source of life—the Holy Spirit (Acts 1:4-8; Gal. 5:13-18). We live a new lifestyle of love (Matt. 22:34-40; Jn. 13:34,35). With our new Lord comes a new occupation—we are ambassadors of the King (1 Cor. 6:19,20; 2 Cor. 5:16-21).

For believers, life should now become an ever-increasing experience of the Kingdom of God. We "are being transformed into his likeness with ever-increasing glory..." (2 Cor. 3:18). As this occurs we also enjoy an ever-increasing experience of *shalom*, that fourfold harmony of relationships seen in the garden.

This experience, however, is an incomplete one. While the kingdom of God was fully present in Jesus and is currently present in the Holy Spirit, our obedience to the Spirit is not perfect. Consequently, like Israel, our experience of the kingdom is imperfect and incomplete. Even as we grow in our relationship with God and in our obedience to his truth, we wait eagerly for something else (Eph. 1:14; Rom. 8:22-25).

Citizens of Two Kingdoms

In this time between Christ's first and second comings, we carry a dual citizenship. We are already citizens of the kingdom of God, yet still live on an earth that is under the curse of sin. We are very much like the children of Israel after Mount Sinai but before the promised land. Because of their disobedience, they had to wander in the desert, known as the "Wilderness of Sin," for forty years before entering the promised land. Likewise, we have established our spiritual citizenship in the kingdom of God, but still live physically in the midst of a similar "wilderness of sin!" Satan has been defeated, but is not yet banished.

This present age is a time of continuing conflict between these two kingdoms, the kingdom of God and the kingdom of the world. Although Satan has been defeated, he still retains dominion over much of creation through deception. He knows that his time is short, and is "filled with fury" and has "blinded the minds of unbelievers" (2 Cor. 4:4). Even against those who have put their faith in Jesus, he has not given up the fight. He "makes war against ... those who obey God's commandments and hold to the testimony of Jesus" (Rev. 12:17).

But he will not succeed! The Church will declare in word and deed the glory of the kingdom of God, and will prevail against him (Matt. 16:18)! The victory has already been won and will someday be fully realized.

Christ's Second Coming—Judgment

The evil and injustice of this present age will one day give way to the justice of Almighty God. A new day is coming, the age of FULLNESS. When Jesus returns, this present world will give way to a new world: "The kingdom of the world has become the kingdom of our Lord and of his Christ, and he will reign for ever and ever" (Rev. 11:15). The second horizontal line in our diagram comes to an end!

Those who have refused to come to Jesus will receive the only appropriate consequence of their decision: they will be banished forever from the presence of God (Rev. 20:10-15). This is another reality that many people today have problems with: "How could a loving God send someone to hell?" they ask.

The truth is that God does not send anyone to hell—he has actually given us a way to avoid it. For those who refuse to acknowledge God and live in his presence today, would it be right to force them to spend eternity with God? Would it not be justice and respecting of their free will to let them experience in eternity what they have chosen throughout their earthly lives—to be separated from God?

Believers, on the other hand, will be received into a new world, into the fullness of life as God intended from the beginning. At this point, everything that God has promised will be experienced in complete fulfillment. God will reign supreme, and *shalom* will be the order of his kingdom! (Rev. 21:1-7). The way to the tree of life will again be wide open (Rev. 22:12-14)!

The conclusion of the matter has been well summed up by George Eldon Ladd:

> And so the Bible ends, with a redeemed society dwelling on a new earth that has been purged of all evil, with God dwelling in the midst of His people. This is the goal of the long course of redemptive history.[8]

Now that we have an overall picture of the kingdom of God, we are ready to turn to the question raised at the end of Chapter Two: what specifically is the *good news* of the kingdom that Jesus spoke about?

Chapter 4

The Good News of the Kingdom

> Because of his great love for us, God, who is rich in mercy, made us alive with Christ even when we were dead in transgressions—it is by grace you have been saved. And God raised us up with Christ and seated us with him in the heavenly realms in Christ Jesus... (Ephesians 2:4-6)

In Chapter Two we looked first at the artificial gospels that have arisen in the church today and then at the genuine one taught by Jesus, the gospel of the kingdom. We also noted the tragedy of artificial gospels in that they fail to transform broken and fragmented lives into the wholesome and integrated lives God designed for us to live. On the other hand, whenever the genuine gospel is proclaimed and lived out, God's power is released to transform individual lives, local churches, communities, and even entire nations.

We also noted these artificial gospels, called "different gospels" by Paul, often result from our oversimplification of the gospel of the kingdom proclaimed by Jesus and the early church. Our motivation has been right: we don't want to make the gospel so complicated that people have a hard time understanding it. The results, however, have often been less than good news.

Perhaps no other passage of scripture has been used by evangelical Christians more frequently in presenting the gospel than Ephesians 2:8,9:

> For it is by grace you have been saved, through faith—and this not from yourselves, it is the gift of God—not by works, so that no one can boast.

These two verses contain very important truth. However, if used by themselves they present an incomplete version of the gospel. It is doubly unfortunate when these two verses alone are presented as the gospel. Not only is the message incomplete and consequently misleading, we also miss a beautiful presentation of the gospel of the kingdom when we look at the *whole* of this chapter! Let's now use this entire second chapter of Paul's letter to the Ephesian church to follow in the footsteps of Philip and present "the things concerning the kingdom of God and the name of Jesus Christ" (Acts 8:12).

But first, let's establish a brief definition of the gospel of the kingdom based on the broad picture of the kingdom of God presented in the previous chapter. We can now define the good news of the kingdom in three statements:

1. **Our Problem:** We were alienated from God by our self-centered attitude and living, held in bondage to sin and Satan.
2. **God's Provision:** But God, out of his love, mercy, and grace, sent Jesus to demonstrate kingdom living and to pay the penalty of our sin. This opened the door for us to answer his call, "Come, follow me!"—setting us free to serve God and reign with him in his kingdom.

3. **Our Privilege:** God sent the Holy Spirit, empowering us to realize our God-given destiny in the context of the Church, the household of God.

Let's now look at how the second chapter of Ephesians presents this good news of the kingdom.

1. Our Problem

Definition:

We were alienated from God by our self-centered attitude and living, held in bondage to sin and Satan.

Ephesians 2:

As for you, you were dead in your transgressions and sins, in which you used to live when you followed the ways of this world and of the ruler of the kingdom of the air, the spirit who is now at work in those who are disobedient. All of us also lived among them at one time, gratifying the cravings of our sinful nature and following its desires and thoughts. Like the rest, we were by nature objects of wrath. (vs. 1-3)

Good News Starts With a Problem?

It may seem strange to begin a definition of "good news" by starting with a problem. How can identifying a problem be good news? Well, if you were on a journey somewhere and had unknowingly lost your way, would that be a problem? And, wouldn't it be good news to discover the problem so that you could take corrective measures?

Seldom do people seek a solution unless they understand there is a problem. Moreover, it's crucial that they understand the *nature* of the problem. Otherwise, they are likely to look for the solution in all the wrong places.

This is precisely the predicament in which the dominant Western culture of our day finds itself. When asked the nature of the problem, our culture typically responds in one of two ways: Either "What problem? There is no problem!" or "The problem is with the system ... or with other people ... or the economy ... or the government ... or religious fanatics ... just anywhere else than with *me*!"

The two dominant, primary cultures of today, modern and postmodern, are both human-centered ones that have dismissed God and his Word, and concluded that the human self is the creative source of life and ultimate authority. And, if we embrace these ideas, we have to place the problem *outside* ourselves. That's why we see a "victim mindset" everywhere we look. Unfortunately, this same mindset has invaded the church to a large degree. Remember the words of Alan Wolfe from Chapter Two: "American faith has met American culture—and American culture has triumphed."[1]

As I have observed the focus of ministry over the last 25 years, we have moved more and more away from the confession and repentance of sin called for in the New Testament, and more towards "healing of past hurts." I realize the sins of others against us impact our lives in a negative way, and that God's provision for this is healing. But things are out of balance. Too often the victim mindset of our culture has been dressed up in spiritual terms and brought into the church. The tragedy is that this often proves to be a "different gospel that is really no gospel at all" (Gal. 1:7), one that is not good news. It leaves people stuck in their sin and dysfunction—looking in the wrong places for the solution to their problems.

The Root Problem
The Word of God sees the problem quite differently than does our culture, as we saw in the previous chapter. The Sin behind our sins—the root that bears bad fruit—is our desire to live independently of God, doing our own thing. And, Paul's words leave no one out: "All of us also lived among them at one time, gratifying the cravings of our sinful nature and following its desires and thoughts" (2:3). We have *all* followed in the footsteps of Adam and Eve, following the "ruler of the kingdom of the air, the spirit who is now at work in those who are disobedient." Paul writes in Romans that we were in such bondage that we were actually "slaves to sin" (6:17).

Like Paul, Jesus also saw things differently than our culture does. He asserted that, while there was a thief who came "only to steal and kill and destroy," he came for a different purpose: "I have come that they may have life, and have it to the full" (Jn. 10:10). And, to him, the way to this "life to the full" was not the pursuit of self-fulfillment, self-actualization, or self-confidence; it was actually grounded in self-denial—so that people would be free from bondage to themselves to follow him and experience his kingdom:

> "If anyone would come after me, he must deny himself and take up his cross daily and follow me. For whoever wants to save his life will lose it, but whoever loses his life for me will save it. What good is it for a man to gain the whole world, and yet lose or forfeit his very self? (Lu. 9:23-25)

The Wrath of God
The last sentence in the Ephesians passage above is hard for us to grasp in today's world: "We were by nature objects of wrath." How can we reconcile God's love and his wrath? To us these are opposites. Paul gives us insight into this in the first

chapter of Romans; "The wrath of God is being revealed from heaven against all the godlessness and wickedness of men who suppress the truth by their wickedness" (v. 18). How was this happening at the time? Were people being struck down by a plague or a similar divine punishment? Not that we have record of.

In the rest of the first chapter of Romans, Paul writes of all the sinful attitudes and behaviors that were happening at the time. In this context, three times he writes that God "gave them over" (v. 24,26,28). He gave them over to "sinful desires," "shameful lusts," and, ultimately, to a "depraved mind."

In other words, God's wrath was revealed when he simply gave people over to the just consequences of their own choices. They wanted to live independently of God; he allowed them to experience what that is like. There is a proverb that gives this same picture of God's wrath: "The mouth of an adulteress is a deep pit; he who is under the LORD'S wrath will fall into it" (Prov. 22:14). When people turn their backs on God, at some point he withdraws his hand of mercy, and they experience the consequences of their sin—they fall into a deep pit.

Time for a Change

We should ask the question, "Has this focus on self in our culture over the last fifty years brought more *shalom* into our lives—into our relationship with God, with ourselves, with others, or with the physical world itself? If not, maybe we should accept what Jesus and Paul are saying—that living self-centered lives is the problem, not the solution! Indeed, the thief Jesus talked about has stolen much through a philosophy of life based on finding health and happiness within oneself, apart from God. Isn't it time for a change?

2. God's Provision

Definition:

> But God, in his love, mercy, and grace, sent Jesus to demonstrate kingdom living and to pay the penalty of our sin. This opened the door for us to answer his call, "Come, follow me!"—setting us free to serve God and reign with him in his kingdom.

Ephesians 2:

> But because of his great love for us, God, who is rich in mercy, made us alive with Christ even when we were dead in transgressions—it is by grace you have been saved. And God raised us up with Christ and seated us with him in the heavenly realms in Christ Jesus, in order that in the coming ages he might show the incomparable riches of his grace, expressed in his kindness to us in Christ Jesus. For it is by grace you have been saved, through faith—and this not from yourselves, it is the gift of God—not by works, so that no one can boast. (vs. 4-9)

The God Who Pursues

The previous section was the bad news about our condition apart from God. And, like Adam and Eve in the Garden, when we become aware of our rebellion against him, our first instinct is to hide. The good news of this section is that, even while we run and hide, God pursues us! God truly is the "Hound of Heaven," as Francis Thompson wrote many years ago in his poem by that name:

> I fled Him, down the nights and down the days;
> I fled Him, down the arches of the years;
> I fled Him, down the labyrinthine ways
>   Of my own mind; and in the mist of tears
> I hid from Him, and under running laughter.
>   Up vistaed hopes I sped;
>   And shot, precipitated,
> Adown Titanic glooms of chasmèd fears,
> From those strong Feet that followed, followed after.
>   But with unhurrying chase,
>   And unperturbèd pace,
>   Deliberate speed, majestic instancy,
>   They beat — and a voice beat
>   More instant than the Feet —
> "All things betray thee, who betrayest Me."

We can run but we can't hide. Our own actions—even our running—will betray us. The lyrics of a favorite song of mine, also from long ago, express this same reality of the God who pursues us:

> I sought the Lord,
>   and afterward I knew
> He moved my soul to seek him,
>   seeking me;
> It was not I that found,
>   O Savior true,
> No, I was found of Thee.[2]

No sooner had human rebellion in the Garden ripped opened the breach in our relationship with God than God's love proclaimed his plan: One would be born of woman who would crush Satan and repair the breach, restoring the relationship. That One would be Jesus. His coming would be the climax of all history:

> When the time had fully come, God sent his Son, born of a woman, born under law, to redeem those under law, that we might receive the full rights of sons. (Gal. 4:4,5)

What are the "full rights of sons?" It would be an enormous task to identify *all* the rights of sons and daughters. Certainly *two* of them would be a relationship with the Father and an inheritance! We will look at the first of these in this section, and then come back to the second later.

God's Loving Mercy

"But because of his great love for us, God, who is rich in mercy...." Before we can understand God's mercy, there is another of his attributes we must understand: "The LORD Almighty will be exalted by his justice, and the holy God will show himself holy by his righteousness" (Isa. 5:16). God is a God of justice and righteousness, and we live in a moral universe. Sin has its consequences. If not in this life, justice will prevail in eternity: "For he has set a day when he will judge the world with justice by the man he has appointed. He has given proof of this to all men by raising him from the dead" (Acts 17:31).

Because of God's justice, we deserve nothing but judgment, for we are all guilty before God: "For all have sinned and fall short of the glory of God" (Rom. 3:23). *But in his mercy, God spares us from what we deserve.* We can picture his mercy as his hand shielding us from what should be ours according to justice. Because of his love he has extended mercy, and "Mercy triumphs over judgment!" (Jas. 2:13).

This does not mean that God could just decide to overlook sin. He could extend mercy only on the basis that Jesus willingly gave himself on our behalf to satisfy God's justice:

> God presented him as a sacrifice of atonement, through faith in his blood. He did this to demonstrate his justice, because in his forbearance he had left the sins committed beforehand unpunished—he did it to demonstrate his justice at the present time, so as to be just and the one who justifies those who have faith in Jesus (Rom. 3:25).

People still have a choice to make. They can accept the fact that Jesus paid the price of their sin and embrace him. Or, they are free to reject him—and pay the price themselves. One way or another, justice requires that the price be paid. Praise be to God for his mercy to us in Christ!

God's Grace
But God's love did not stop with his mercy. *In his grace God goes beyond mercy and gives us what we don't deserve:* "God ... made us alive with Christ even when we were dead in transgressions—it is by grace you have been saved." This saving grace comes to us "through faith—and this not from yourselves, it is the gift of God—not by works, so that no one can boast" (2:8,9). As a popular song a few years back declared, "Even the faith comes from You!" As we simply turn from our running and embrace God in sincerity and humility, God births faith in our spirit—the faith to take hold of the good news of the kingdom of God and the Lord Jesus.

Our salvation is not something that can be earned by our works; neither is faith something that we can conjure up within us. Both are gifts from God. As we soften our hearts toward God, the Holy Spirit convicts us of our sin, draws us to God, and pours out his gifts upon us as we embrace him and yield to his kingdom.

As we turn towards God and faith rises within us, God makes us "alive with Christ." Spiritual death was the result of the breach of relationship between God and us that was caused by our sin. Spiritual life is the result of that relationship being restored as our sin is forgiven because of the sacrifice of Christ on our behalf. The life of God now begins to flow into our lives once again, bringing with it many new possibilities, as we have already seen.

Seated With Christ
Too often people—especially evangelical Christians—treat verses six and seven of the second chapter of Ephesians as an unnecessary interlude between verses five and eight. Nothing could be further from the truth!

Not only have we been given new life, but we have a new position as well: "And God raised us up with Christ and seated us with him in the heavenly realms in Christ Jesus...." (Ephesians 2:6). If we fail to understand the significance of this, we will fail to understand a very important aspect of the gospel of the kingdom.

Kings take their seat on a throne to rule. To be seated is to embrace their position of authority. Jesus is now seated at the right hand of the Father, reigning as the King of Kings and Lord of Lords (Heb. 12:2; Rev. 19:16). *And we are seated with him!* God seated us there for a purpose—he wanted us to reclaim the destiny given us in creation: to reign with him in his kingdom.

Is this just a picture of something that will be realized in the future, or is this a *present* reality that can make a difference in our everyday lives? To answer that question, let's review what a "kingdom" actually is.

We Each Have a Kingdom
We have defined a kingdom as, "a sphere of influence in which a king rules." We went on to see that, in creation, God gave us free will—the right, ability and responsibility to make our own decisions. So, it is proper to say that each of us has a "kingdom." We each make decisions each day about how we will live out our lives. In our work or ministry, we may also have areas in which our decisions are final. Whatever the case, all that falls within that realm in which we have the responsibility and the legitimate right to make decisions is a part of our "kingdom," our sphere of influence.

Dallas Willard has pointed out that having a "kingdom" is at the heart of our own personhood.[3] God created us as spiritual beings and gave us the ability and the freedom to make decisions about our own life. This is what sets human beings apart from the rest of God's creation, and is the essence of personhood. "God created human beings; he created them godlike, reflecting God's nature. He created them male and female" (Gen. 1:27, *The Message*). Nothing remotely close to this is said about any other part of God's creation.

Nothing destroys our sense of personhood more than when another person violates the free will that God gave us by making our decisions for us, controlling and manipulating us to do their will rather than our own. If you have ever encountered a person who was almost totally controlled by another person, you know it is not a pretty thing to lose one's sense of personhood. God, who gave us our free will, does not violate our "kingdom." Neither should anyone else!

But we need to add a couple of qualifiers here. First, parents of minor children have the legitimate right to make those decisions for their children which the children are not mature enough to make for themselves. But even here, parents are wise to give their children safe boundaries and allow them to make decisions within those boundaries. When children arrive at the age of adulthood, we want them to know how to make wise decisions, not how to find someone else to make their decisions for them.

Second, God has ordained the state to maintain order when people refuse to act orderly (Rom. 13:1-5). Persons who violate the law and end up in prison have given up the right to make a lot of their own decisions. However, both in this case and in the case of minor children, they still retain the right to decide for or against cooperation with their guardians. They can choose not to cooperate, though in so doing they are also choosing to accept the consequences. One of the greatest of all learning experiences is that our decisions have consequences.

Regaining Our Competency to Rule
As we have already seen, at creation God gave the human race the responsibility to reign over the rest of his creation—but only as we ourselves submit to his reign over us. It is only in this context that we are competent to fulfill our assignment. From Roman culture to postmodern culture, people who have attempted to live independently of God, have "trivialized themselves into silliness and confusion so that there was neither sense nor direction left in their lives" (Rom. 1:21, *The Message*). They still have the desire to "be in charge," but do not have the competency to do so in an effective way.

Living apart from a vital relationship with God has other fallout as well. Because God is the author of life and we were created in his image, it is impossible to maintain a proper respect for life apart from a proper respect for God. Life tends to lose its meaning for us and we tend to lose a proper respect for other people. Consequently, our relationships are impacted: they end up inclined more toward discord than harmony, as we have seen. The end result is that life becomes a struggle among incompetent, competing "kingdoms" at every level of society. This is true for individuals, families, communities, and nations—unfortunately even for many churches!

Now that we have seen the downside of living independently of God, we are ready for the "good news of the kingdom!" When our relationship with God is restored and we are "raised up with Christ and seated with him in the heavenly realms" *our competency to rule is restored!* As we submit our kingdoms to his, we can now see order and purpose restored to our lives—to our "kingdoms." With Christ, "all things are possible" (Matt. 19:26). With Paul, we can say, "I can do everything through him who gives me strength" (Phil. 4:13). We no longer need to see ourselves as helpless victims.

Restoring Order and Harmony

When we understand this, we will quit looking in all the wrong places for the solutions to life's problems. When we experience dysfunction in our lives, we will ask God, "What is the problem here and how do you want to bring order and harmony back into this part of my kingdom?"

In many cases, we will need to confront, confess, and repent of sin in our lives. When we do so, we will discover what David discovered long ago:

> When I kept silent, my bones wasted away through my groaning all day long. For day and night your hand was heavy upon me; my strength was sapped as in the heat of summer.
> Then I acknowledged my sin to you and did not cover up my iniquity. I said, "I will confess my transgressions to the LORD"—and you forgave the guilt of my sin. (Ps. 32:3-5)

All sin impacts lives. As a friend of mine once said, "When someone sins, someone suffers." Our own sin impacts our lives and the lives of others. In turn, the sins of others against us also impact our lives. When this happens, we will need to confront others with their wrongful attitudes or actions—but when we do so, it will be done out of a proper respect for them and out of a desire to see order and harmony come to *their* kingdoms, as well:

> If your brother sins, rebuke him, and if he repents, forgive him. If he sins against you seven times in a day, and seven times comes back to you and says, "I repent," forgive him. (Lu. 17:3,4)

> If someone is caught in a sin, you who are spiritual should restore him gently. But watch yourself, or you also may be tempted. Carry each other's burdens, and in this way you will fulfill the law of Christ. (Gal. 6:1,2)

Many times, we will find that dysfunction in our lives is simply the result of failing to nurture the life of Christ within us—we have failed to grow up spiritually. We have neglected Peter's advice: "Like newborn babies, crave pure spiritual milk, so that by it you may grow up in your salvation, now that you have tasted that the Lord is good" (1 Pet. 2:2). We will discuss this further in Chapter Eight.

Seated With a Purpose

Ephesians 2:7 begins with the words, "in order that," implying that God had a clear purpose in mind when he seated us with Christ and restored our competency to reign with him: "...in order that in the coming ages he might show the incomparable riches of his grace, expressed in his kindness to us in Christ Jesus."

God's plan has always been to work though his people to bring blessing to his world. We have the same calling as did Abraham—we are "blessed to be a blessing." As our kingdoms are brought into order under his kingdom, "the incomparable riches of his grace" are expressed in his kindness to us and passed on to others. What a blessing it is to serve God's purposes in his kingdom, to be a channel of his grace and kindness to others!

But these blessings are available to us as a privilege, not as an automatic download; we must actively take hold of them if they are to be realized in our lives and in the lives of those to whom we minister. It is to this privilege that we turn for the concluding section of this chapter.

3. Our Privilege

Definition:

> God sent the Holy Spirit, empowering us to realize our God-given destiny in the context of the Church, the household of God.

Ephesians 2:

> We are God's workmanship, created in Christ Jesus to do good works, which God prepared in advance for us to do. (v.10)
>
> Now in Christ Jesus you who once were far away have been brought near through the blood of Christ. For he himself is our peace, who has made the two one and has destroyed the barrier, the dividing wall of hostility... His purpose was to create in himself one new man out of the two, thus making peace, and in this one body to reconcile both of them to God through

the cross, by which he put to death their hostility. (vs. 13-16)

Consequently, you are no longer foreigners and aliens, but fellow citizens with God's people and members of God's household, built on the foundation of the apostles and prophets, with Christ Jesus himself as the chief cornerstone. In him the whole building is joined together and rises to become a holy temple in the Lord. And in him you too are being built together to become a dwelling in which God lives by his Spirit. (vs. 19-22)

There are great blessings available to us as sons and daughters of God—a rich inheritance. As Paul gave his farewell address to the elders of the church in Ephesus, he spoke these words: "Now I commit you to God and to the word of his grace, which can build you up and give you an inheritance among all those who are sanctified" (Acts 20:32). Let's look at the inheritance God has given us as his children.

We Have a Destiny
Just as Ephesians 2:6,7 are often overlooked between verses five and eight, so many times people stop after verse nine. Again, verse 10 begins with the connector, "For." In other words, what comes after is the purpose for what came before. We have been saved "by grace through faith," not by works—yet we have been saved "to do good works, which God prepared in advance for us to do."

God has given us a destiny—designed for us even before we were born. A particular part of God's kingdom was set aside for us over which to reign with Christ, as we do the "good works" required for the proper functioning of that particular "province" of the kingdom. And, we are not left alone to do this with our own limited resources.

Before Jesus finished his work here on earth and returned to Father God in heaven, he said, "I will not leave you as orphans; I will come to you.... the Holy Spirit, whom the Father will send in my name, will teach you all things and will remind you of everything I have said to you" (Jn. 14:18,26). It is by this Holy Spirit that we now have access to the Father (Eph. 2:18). Accordingly, the resources of heaven—God's power and authority—are available to us on earth. It is only because of this that Jesus could teach his disciples to pray, "Our Father in heaven, hallowed be your name, your kingdom come, your will be done *on earth* as it is in heaven" (Matt. 6:9,10, emphasis added).

God's New Community
The Holy Spirit is now at work, taking our individual "provinces" of the kingdom and molding them into one body. As we are reconciled to God, this reconciliation spills over into our relationships with others, destroying the hostility that has kept us apart. In this way, God's new community is created— the alternative "kingdom culture" that we talked of earlier. As we are joined together, we become "a holy temple in the Lord ... a dwelling in which God lives by his Spirit" (Eph. 2:21,22). Reconciliation to God and reconciliation to each other fulfills the Great Commandment:

> Love the Lord your God with all your heart and with all your soul and with all your mind." This is the first and greatest commandment. And the second is like it: "Love your neighbor as yourself." All the Law and the Prophets hang on these two commandments (Matt. 22:37-40).

Jesus was clear that this "spill-over" of the Holy Spirit into our relationships with others in God's New Community—the Church—would have a profound impact upon the world:

> I have given them the glory that you gave me, that they may be one as we are one: I in them and you in me. May they be brought to complete unity to let the world know that you sent me and have loved them even as you have loved me (Jn. 17:22,23).

God truly is the center of things, in our experience as well as in our theology. When our relationship with him is not right, all of life is impacted. When this relationship is restored, the potential for life as intended from the beginning is restored. We have called this *shalom*. Out of our living relationship with God flows emotional and physical health and healthy, fulfilling relationships with others. Others will see and take notice. We will demonstrate to them an authentic kingdom culture as an alternative to all the artificial cultures of our world.

Revealing the Glory of God

As this happens, we are "being transformed into his likeness with ever-increasing glory, which comes from the Lord, who is the Spirit" (2 Cor. 3:18). Note this is an "ever-increasing glory." This transformation is a lifelong process. It will only be completed when Jesus returns or we go to be with him.

However, we have the privilege *now* of experiencing substantial transformation in our lives—spiritually, emotionally, socially, and physically. As we experience this, we will be revealers of God's glory to those around us, demonstrating the wholesome, integrated life God designed from the beginning. What an awesome opportunity!

In this chapter we have endeavored to define the good news of the kingdom, the genuine gospel that brings transformation. In the next chapter, we will take a closer look at how this good news connects with our lives in such a way that God is able to transform our lives and the entire "province" of the kingdom that God has assigned to us.

Chapter 5

The Process of Transformation

Do not conform any longer to the pattern of this world, but be transformed by the renewing of your mind... (Romans 12:2)

Now the Lord is the Spirit, and where the Spirit of the Lord is, there is freedom. And we, who with unveiled faces all reflect the Lord's glory, are being transformed into his likeness with ever-increasing glory, which comes from the Lord, who is the Spirit. (2 Corinthians 3:17,18)

There is an old saying that asks: "How do you eat an elephant?" Of course, the answer is, "One bite at a time!" When it comes to the subject of transformation, we can ask a similar question: "How does transformation happen?" The answer is much the same: "One person at a time!"

There is a new awareness in our time that God wants to transform not just individual persons, but whole communities and entire nations. George Otis, Jr. has documented a number of different communities around the world where God has been working in amazing ways.[1] Without question, it's exciting to think about entire communities being transformed by the power of God. But we must remember that God has always chosen to work through individual persons who hear and answer his call to service in the kingdom of God—and who touch the lives of others.

Transformed persons make up transformed churches. Transformed churches are used by God to transform their communities and beyond. However, as we have seen, the research of George Gallup, Jr., and George Barna shows the Western church to be in need of much transformation itself. If we expect to see significant transformation in our communities without addressing the desperate need for transformation in our churches—and within the individual lives that make up those churches—we will be set up for disappointment.

In the previous two chapters we looked at an overview of the kingdom of God and saw how Paul presented the good news of Jesus and the kingdom of God to the Ephesians. Now we want to ask the question, "How does God connect this good news to individual lives in such a way that the power of God is unleashed to produce transformed lives?"

To get a clear, comprehensive understanding of this process, we will begin with the *call* of Jesus to the first-century disciples. Then, we will look at three biblical phrases, all of which have been used individually to describe the way we respond to the call of Jesus and enter into a transforming relationship with him. If we take them all together, we get a clear and compelling picture of a journey that truly brings transformation.

The Call of Jesus

The writer of the letter to the Hebrews wrote, "Jesus Christ is the same yesterday and today and forever" (Heb. 13:8). That being true, we can be sure his call to us is the same call he issued in the first century. As he was walking on the shore of the Sea of Galilee and encountered the fishermen Simon Peter and his brother Andrew, his call to them was, "Come, follow me, and I will make you fishers of men." Their response was immediate: "They left their nets and followed him" (Matt. 4:19,20).

As he came upon Matthew sitting at the tax collector's booth, he simply said, "Follow me," and Matthew got up and followed him (Matt. 9:9). The same call came to Philip in John 1:43. It's a simple call, and some times we get the impression from the responses of Peter, Andrew, Matthew, Philip and others that it is a simple response.

But it's also clear that the call of Jesus to "Follow me" required a significant choice to leave behind anything that would get in the way of following. Not everyone was ready to do it. When Jesus came to a young man of great wealth, he said, "If you want to be perfect, go, sell your possessions and give to the poor, and you will have treasure in heaven. Then come, follow me" (Matt. 19:21). This young man's response was different: "He went away sad, because he had great wealth" (Matt. 19:22).

In fact, Jesus made it clear that for *anyone* to follow him, something would need to be left behind:

> If anyone would come after me, he must deny himself and take up his cross and follow me. For whoever wants to save his life will lose it, but whoever loses his life for me will find it. What good will it be for a man if he gains the whole world, yet forfeits his soul? Or what can a man give in exchange for his soul? (Matt. 16:24-26).

The call of Jesus to "Follow me" was not an extension of a massive ego that needed to be gratified by having followers. His call was "Follow me" because to follow in his footsteps was to find genuine, authentic life as God intended it and as Jesus was experiencing it. The thief had already come and stolen this from the earth; now Jesus was here to restore it: "The thief comes only to steal and kill and destroy; I have come that they may have life, and have it to the full" (Jn. 10:10).

This is why the call involved laying something aside. As we have seen in our definition of the gospel of the kingdom, at the heart of our alienation from God is our self-centered attitudes and living. Jesus knows what is in the hearts of those he calls, and he knows those desires and priorities that would prevent us from experiencing life to the full if they were to remain. And, at the core of all these roadblocks to kingdom living is the same problem—the desire to live independently of God.

For Peter and Andrew, if fishing had remained priority number one in their lives, they would never have been able to follow the call of Jesus to a different kind of fishing. For the rich young man, his wealth would have always been a roadblock on the road to fullness of life—that's why Jesus called him to lay it aside. The wealthy young man was not the only one to go away from this encounter with Jesus sad; I'm sure that Jesus also went away sad, knowing the man was missing his opportunity for life in all its fullness.

This does not mean that wealth is always a problem. One of the first books I remember reading as a young boy was entitled *God Runs My Business*, the story of R. G. LeTourneau (1888-1969), one of my dad's heroes of the faith. LeTourneau was a great industrialist, inventor and business man. He was responsible for nearly 300 patents, and the mammoth machines he built represented nearly 70% of the earthmoving equipment used during World War II.

The thing I remember most about the book was that, throughout his adult life, LeTourneau gave away 90% of his wealth and lived on 10%. Jesus would not have called him to lay down his wealth because it was not an obstacle to his experience of the kingdom of God—it was, in fact, a blessing to the kingdom that God could use to bless many others.

Before going on, we must ask a very important question: How does the call of Jesus come to *us* today? When Jesus lived physically on this earth, the call came as he spoke it personally. But while God is present with us by his Holy Spirit today, Jesus is not here in bodily form to present the call in the same manner that he did when he walked the earth.

The answer to our question can be found in Paul's letter to the Romans:

> Scripture reassures us, "No one who trusts God like this—heart and soul—will ever regret it." It's exactly the same no matter what a person's religious background may be: the same God for all of us, acting the same incredibly generous way to everyone who calls out for help. "Everyone who calls, 'Help, God!' gets help."
>
> But how can people call for help if they don't know who to trust? And how can they know who to trust if they haven't heard of the One who can be trusted? And how can they hear if nobody tells them? And how is anyone going to tell them, unless someone is sent to do it?
>
> That's why Scripture exclaims, "A sight to take your breath away! Grand processions of people telling all the good things of God!"

But not everybody is ready for this, ready to see and hear and act. Isaiah asked what we all ask at one time or another: "Does anyone care, God? Is anyone listening and believing a word of it?" The point is, Before you trust, you have to listen. But unless Christ's Word is preached, there's nothing to listen to. (Rom. 10:11-16, *The Message*)

Clearly, the call of Jesus comes to us as we hear Christ's message proclaimed, as it is recorded in God's Word. Usually this comes through persons who are faithful to the call of Christ on their lives and who share the message with us. But there are also testimonies of persons who simply picked up the Scriptures, started reading, and the Holy Spirit delivered the call directly.

The journey to transformation always begins with the call of Jesus to "Come, follow me." Jesus clearly expects those who would respond to him to actually follow him in everyday life—to do what he would do in the situation and experience life as it was intended to be—*shalom*. This is why Paul wrote to the Corinthian Christians, "Follow my example, as I follow the example of Christ" (1 Cor. 11:1).

At the core of our response to the call of Jesus is a change of allegiance—we turn away from self as the center of life and confess, "Jesus is Lord!" As we have seen, to be free to follow always involves laying something down, yielding our will to God's. But we can't do this without God's help. Jesus said, "No one can come to me unless the Father who sent me draws him" (John 6:44). How does God draw us to him? He sends his Spirit to bring conviction:

It's better for you that I leave. If I don't leave, the Friend won't come. But if I go, I'll send him to you.

> "When he comes, he'll expose the error of the godless world's view of sin, righteousness, and judgment: He'll show them that their refusal to believe in me is their basic sin; that righteousness comes from above, where I am with the Father, out of their sight and control; that judgment takes place as the ruler of this godless world is brought to trial and convicted. (Jn. 16:7-11, *The Message*)

We will now turn to the three biblical phrases referred to at the beginning of this chapter. Taken together, they give us a clear picture of how the good news of the kingdom and the convicting work of the Word and the Spirit connect with our lives to transform us "into his likeness with ever-increasing glory."

1. Repent and be converted
2. You must be born again
3. What must I do to be saved?

To avoid any confusion, we should note that these three phrases describe three aspects of a continuing journey, not three distinct steps of a religious "formula."

Three Biblical Phrases

1. "Repent and Be Converted"

> Repent therefore and be converted, that your sins may be blotted out, so that times of refreshing may come from the presence of the Lord, and that He may send Jesus Christ, who was preached to you before, whom heaven must receive until the times of restoration of all things, which God has spoken by the mouth

of all His holy prophets since the world began. (Acts 3:19-21, NKJV).

Peter was addressing the crowd that had come to the temple for afternoon prayers—and who had just witnessed the dramatic healing of a man crippled from birth. This man who had been brought to the temple to beg asked Peter and John for money. Peter's answer was straightforward: "Silver or gold I do not have, but what I have I give you. In the name of Jesus Christ of Nazareth, walk" (Acts 3:6). What followed was a powerful demonstration of the kingdom of God invading the kingdom of this world.

Peter took the man by the hand, pulled him to his feet, and instantly his feet and ankles became strong and he began to walk and jump and praise God! To the amazed crowd, Peter then explained how this happened:

> Men of Israel, why does this surprise you? Why do you stare at us as if by our own power or godliness we had made this man walk....By faith in the name of Jesus, this man whom you see and know was made strong. It is Jesus' name and the faith that comes through him that has given this complete healing to him, as you can all see. (Acts 3:6,16)

He then admonished them with a command—a call to take responsive action to the power of God they had just witnessed: "Repent and be converted..." It was not just a suggestion; it was what *must* happen if they were to have their sins blotted out so they could experience the refreshing presence of God and his kingdom.

Repentance is often thought of in our day as a sorrowful feeling about our sins—or at least sorrow about our sins being found out. It's true there is often an element of sorrow attached to repentance, but it is a different kind of sorrow: "Godly sorrow brings repentance that leads to salvation and leaves no regret, but worldly sorrow brings death" (2 Cor. 7:10). Godly sorrow comes from the conviction of the Holy Spirit that we have sinned against God and leads us to repentance. Repentance, then, is not the sorrow: it is our response to the godly sorrow.

If we look at the original Greek words for "repent" and "be converted" in this passage, we get a clear picture of what biblical repentance actually is. The original word for repent is *metanoeō*, meaning "to change your mind." The word translated "be converted" means "to turn back." The two taken together would literally say "change your mind and turn back."

In the Hebrew language of the Old Testament, both of these words are wrapped up in the word *shub*, simply meaning "to turn back." The difference is that Hebrew is a concrete language—you know if there has been a change of mind by the change in direction one takes. It is inconceivable in Hebrew culture and language that people could change their mind without changing their direction.

Greek and English are abstract languages, however. We have no problem talking about abstract concepts apart from any concrete action. We often talk about "having faith" apart from any resulting action, for example. In contrast, in Hebrew there is no concept or word for "faith" apart from "faithfulness."

So, given all this, how would we define "repentance" in a way that would faithfully communicate to us the biblical understanding?

Biblical repentance is a change of mind resulting in a two-fold change in direction—to God and from sin:

1. You know that I have not hesitated to preach anything that would be helpful to you but have taught you publicly and from house to house. I have declared to both Jews and Greeks that they must *turn to God in repentance* and have faith in our Lord Jesus. (Acts 20:20,21, emphasis added)

2. Therefore, O house of Israel, I will judge you, each one according to his ways, declares the Sovereign LORD. *Repent! Turn away from all your offenses;* then sin will not be your downfall. Rid yourselves of all the offenses you have committed, and get a new heart and a new spirit. Why will you die, O house of Israel? For I take no pleasure in the death of anyone, declares the Sovereign LORD. Repent and live! (Ezek. 18:30-32, emphasis added)

Paul's writing in Acts 26:20 expresses the validity of this definition:

First to those in Damascus, then to those in Jerusalem and in all Judea, and to the Gentiles also, I preached that they should *repent and turn to God and prove their repentance by their deeds.* (Emphasis added; see Jas. 2:14-26 for further verification)

This understanding of repentance became very clear to me personally in 1994 and 1995. On January 2, 1994, the first Sunday of the New Year, I was up early in the morning walking the floor and praying as I usually do before bringing the morning message. As I prayed, I heard a very clear message in my mind that I knew was from the Lord:

You have been praying for revival, but you need to remember something—The ministry of John the Baptist preceded My ministry. The baptism of repentance preceded the baptism of the Holy Spirit. And *a season of repentance must precede a season of revival.*

It was just eighteen days later, on January 20, 1994, that a move of God began at what is now Airport Christian Fellowship in Toronto, Ontario. From its beginning, the focus of this stirring of God's power has been on turning people's hearts back to Father God. I have made several trips there and have always come back home refreshed and with a deeper love for God.

Then, on Father's Day, June 18, 1995, another move of God burst forth at the Brownsville Assembly of God Church in Pensacola, Florida. From the onset of this move, God has been speaking to people about holiness and turning away from sin. From the first day, people have flocked to the altar to confess their sins when the invitation has been given.

I believe it is very significant that these two moves of God came in the order in which they did. *We truly must turn to God before we can turn away from sin.* As a pastor for many years, I have known people who definitely did not like the results of the sin in their lives, and who tried desperately to turn away from it. However, they refused to change their minds about God and turn to him first, yielding their will to his. Consequently, they remained stuck in the sin and dysfunction in their lives and in the lives of those around them.

The process of transformation is initiated when we hear the call of Jesus to "Come, follow me!" for only as we follow the King can we experience kingdom life, *shalom.* As we hear the call, we experience what the very first Gentiles to hear the message experienced:

> Brothers, you know that some time ago God made a choice among you that the Gentiles might hear from my lips the message of the gospel and believe. God, who knows the heart, showed that he accepted them by giving the Holy Spirit to them, just as he did to us. He made no distinction between us and them, for he purified their hearts by faith. (Acts 15:7-9)

God "knows the heart." When he sees a sincere desire there to follow Jesus, he births faith in us by the Holy Spirit that "purifies" our heart. This divine work of grace stirs us to "repent and be converted." We change our minds about God, turn to God and away from our self-centered thinking and living, pledging our allegiance to Jesus as our Lord and King. In doing so, we are submitting our kingdoms to his.

Along with Peter's admonition to "repent and be converted," came a promised blessing: "that your sins may be blotted out, so that times of refreshing may come from the presence of the Lord...." Without this refreshing and empowering presence of the Lord, we could never truly submit our kingdoms to Jesus and his kingdom. Further understanding of how this comes to us will become evident as we turn to the second of the three phrases.

2. "You Must be Born Again"

> Now there was a man of the Pharisees named Nicodemus, a member of the Jewish ruling council. He came to Jesus at night and said, "Rabbi, we know you are a teacher who has come from God. For no one could perform the miraculous signs you are doing if God were not with him."

In reply Jesus declared, "I tell you the truth, no one can see the kingdom of God unless he is born again."

"How can a man be born when he is old?" Nicodemus asked. "Surely he cannot enter a second time into his mother's womb to be born!"

Jesus answered, "I tell you the truth, no one can enter the kingdom of God unless he is born of water and the Spirit. Flesh gives birth to flesh, but the Spirit gives birth to spirit. You should not be surprised at my saying, 'You must be born again.' The wind blows wherever it pleases. You hear its sound, but you cannot tell where it comes from or where it is going. So it is with everyone born of the Spirit." (Jn. 3:1-8)

As we have seen in the creation account, God put the tree of the knowledge of good and evil off limits to Adam and Eve and said to them, "when you eat of it you will surely die" (Gen. 2:17). When they disobeyed God, death surely came. Physical death did not come immediately, but it was sure to come in due time. A spiritual death took place at once, however. The intimate, relational connection with God was obscured by their rebellious act, as a holy God cannot tolerate the presence of sin: "Your iniquities have separated you from your God; your sins have hidden his face from you, so that he will not hear" (Isa. 59:2).

For Adam and Eve—and for all of us who have followed in their footsteps—when we are living in rebellion against God, we are separated from his empowering life in us. As we have seen, in this condition we are incompetent to carry out his charge to us to rule over the "province" of the kingdom to which we have been assigned—beginning with the management of our own lives.

All the different versions of twelve-step programs around us today acknowledge this reality in one way or another. All recognize that significant and meaningful change can begin when we admit "our lives have become unmanageable." While this may be more visibly evident in lives afflicted with drugs and alcohol, it is nevertheless true across the board—*no one* is able to rule his or her life properly, the way God intended life to work, apart from a living relationship with God. As we come to the story of Nicodemus and his encounter with Jesus in John 3:1-8, we get more insight into this transforming relationship.

As Nicodemus came to Jesus, he acknowledged what was evident to any open-minded person around Jesus: "We know you are a teacher who has come from God. For no one could perform the miraculous signs you are doing if God were not with him." The life of God's kingdom, God's love and his power, were evident in the miracles of transformation Jesus worked in the lives of the people he came in contact with.

Jesus' reply was straight to the point: "I tell you the truth, no one can see the kingdom of God unless he is born again." Because of the spiritual death all of us had suffered due to our rebellion, there was no way this love and power of God, this kingdom life, was going to be present in anyone's life (other than Jesus) apart from a new birth. Of course, Nicodemus could not understand this at all—how could someone enter again into his mother's womb and be born again?

Jesus made clear to him he was talking about a different kind of birth—a spiritual birth. Just as everyone had been "born of water"—meaning a natural, physical birth—now everyone was in need of being "born of the Spirit" because only "the Spirit gives birth to spirit."

The good news of Jesus is that when we quit running from God, turn to him and embrace him by putting our lives in his hands, an amazing thing happens. We are "born of the

Spirit." The life of God himself comes to take up residence in our spirits, again bringing into our lives the ability and competency to reign with God in the sphere of influence he assigns to us.

Paul's prayer for the Ephesians—and for all of us—was that we would come to a deep understanding of the significance of this:

> I pray also that the eyes of your heart may be enlightened in order that you may know the hope to which he has called you, the riches of his glorious inheritance in the saints, and his incomparably great power for us who believe. That power is like the working of his mighty strength, which he exerted in Christ when he raised him from the dead and seated him at his right hand in the heavenly realms, far above all rule and authority, power and dominion, and every title that can be given, not only in the present age but also in the one to come. (Eph. 1:18-21)

When Jesus took our sin upon himself, wiped our slates clean, and sent his Spirit to us, *he opened the door of his kingdom to us.* In Paul's words, he qualified us "to share in the inheritance of the saints in the kingdom of light. For he has rescued us from the dominion of darkness and brought us into the kingdom of the Son he loves" (Col. 1:12,13). Now, by the power of the Spirit, we are free to do what he called us to from the beginning—to reign with him, seated with him on his throne. When we truly understand this, the journey of transformation in our lives is well underway!

In addition to this present power of God in our lives, this gift of the Spirit to us is also the promise that more is to come. Again, in Paul's words to the Ephesian Christians:

> And you also were included in Christ when you heard the word of truth, the gospel of your salvation. Having believed, you were marked in him with a seal, the promised Holy Spirit, who is a deposit guaranteeing our inheritance until the redemption of those who are God's possession—to the praise of his glory. (Eph. 1:13,14)

Paul's words confirm the words Jesus spoke to Nicodemus in their late night encounter, contained in perhaps the most well-known verses in all of Scripture: "For God so loved the world that he gave his one and only Son, that whoever believes in him shall not perish but have eternal life" (John 3:16). This life with Jesus is eternal life—life with no end. We who already have "the firstfruits of the Spirit" (Rom. 8:23) know there is more yet to come, and we wait eagerly for all the fullness of the kingdom of God throughout all eternity, as we saw in Chapter Three.

Before going on to the third of our three phrases, we must look a bit further at our relationship with the Holy Spirit. While a comprehensive study of the work of the Holy Spirit in our lives is beyond the scope of this book, we do need to look at two additional biblical terms concerning the Holy Spirit. In addition to being *born of the Spirit* as we have just seen, the Bible also speaks of being *baptized with the Holy Spirit* and being *filled with the Spirit*. What is the significance of these two terms? There has been much unfortunate debate and division over their meaning during the past century. Let us make every effort to get beyond that in this discussion!

As John the Baptist went about his ministry of preparing the way for Jesus, he preached and practiced a "baptism of repentance for the forgiveness of sins" (Mk. 1:4). But John was not one to call attention to himself. Instead, he pointed ahead to the One who was to follow him:

> After me will come one more powerful than I, the thongs of whose sandals I am not worthy to stoop down and untie. I baptize you with water, but he will baptize you with the Holy Spirit. (Mk. 1:7,8)

During the forty days that Jesus spent with his followers after his resurrection and before he returned to Father God, he gave them these instructions:

> Do not leave Jerusalem, but wait for the gift my Father promised, which you have heard me speak about. For John baptized with water, but in a few days you will be baptized with the Holy Spirit....
>
> You will receive power when the Holy Spirit comes on you; and you will be my witnesses in Jerusalem, and in all Judea and Samaria, and to the ends of the earth. (Acts 1:4,5,8)

If we take this term *baptized with the Spirit* literally, it would mean simply to be immersed with the Spirit. If the believers would follow the instruction of Jesus, he promised they would be immersed in the presence of the Holy Spirit in a new way, a way that would empower them to be his witnesses throughout the earth.

At that point, I expect the believers waiting there in the upper room may have reflected back on an event in the life of Jesus where he spoke of water and the Spirit. One year, Jesus went up to Jerusalem for the celebration of the Feast of Tabernacles. He went into the temple courts and began to teach the people:

> On the last and greatest day of the Feast, Jesus stood and said in a loud voice, "If anyone is thirsty, let him come to me and drink. Whoever believes in me, as the

Scripture has said, streams of living water will flow from within him." By this he meant the Spirit, whom those who believed in him were later to receive. (Jn. 7:37-39)

While not a direct quote from the Scriptures, this is clearly a reference back to Ezekiel's prophecy of the new and eternal temple where God would "live among the Israelites forever" (Ezek. 43:7). Jesus clearly referred to himself as this eternal temple in John 2:18-21:

> Then the Jews demanded of him, "What miraculous sign can you show us to prove your authority to do all this?"
> Jesus answered them, "Destroy this temple, and I will raise it again in three days."
> The Jews replied, "It has taken forty-six years to build this temple, and you are going to raise it in three days?" But the temple he had spoken of was his body.

Now, during the Feast of Tabernacles, this Eternal Temple of God stood in the courts of the temporal one, a structure that was soon to be so thoroughly destroyed by the Romans that "they will not leave one stone on another, because you did not recognize the time of God's coming to you" (Lu. 19:44). With a loud voice, he invited those who were thirsty to put their trust in him and promised "streams of living water" would flow from within them by the Spirit.

There is an incredible picture of this in Ezekiel 47 where the prophet first sees water trickle from under the eastern gate of the temple that soon grew to ankle deep, then knee deep, then waist deep, and finally to a mighty "river that no one could cross" (Ezek. 47:5). But what is truly amazing is what happens wherever this water flows:

> This water flows toward the eastern region and goes down into the Arabah, where it enters the Sea. When it empties into the Sea, the water there becomes fresh. Swarms of living creatures will live wherever the river flows. There will be large numbers of fish, because this water flows there and makes the salt water fresh; so where the river flows everything will live. Fishermen will stand along the shore; from En Gedi to En Eglaim there will be places for spreading nets. The fish will be of many kinds—like the fish of the Great Sea. But the swamps and marshes will not become fresh; they will be left for salt. Fruit trees of all kinds will grow on both banks of the river. Their leaves will not wither, nor will their fruit fail. Every month they will bear, because the water from the sanctuary flows to them. Their fruit will serve for food and their leaves for healing. (Ezek. 47:8-12)

What a picture of transformation that touches everything in its path! Of course, those who choose to stay in the swamps and marshes are left unchanged, but everything else is baptized, or immersed, in the Spirit of God and filled with new life! To this we can only say, "Let the river flow, Lord!"

Now let's look at the second of these two terms, *filled with the Spirit*. That there is a close connection between the two is apparent from the Scriptures. When Jesus promised the encounter that was to come, he said "you will be baptized with the Holy Spirit." When Luke reported the fulfillment of that promise, he wrote, "All of them were filled with the Holy Spirit" (Acts 2:4).

When we think of something being *filled* we imagine pouring something into a cup or other container until it is *full.* Some understand being *filled with the Holy Spirit* in this way. When they have a certain kind of experience with the Holy Spirit, they are then *filled* and remain *Spirit-filled* from that point on.

But it is clear from the New Testament that being *filled with the Holy Spirit* is not a one-time experience. The believers that Jesus left behind when he returned to the Father first received the fulfillment of Jesus' promise as they were gathered together on the Day of Pentecost:

> When the day of Pentecost came, they were all together in one place. Suddenly a sound like the blowing of a violent wind came from heaven and filled the whole house where they were sitting. They saw what seemed to be tongues of fire that separated and came to rest on each of them. All of them were *filled with the Holy Spirit* and began to speak in other tongues as the Spirit enabled them. (Acts 2:1-4, emphasis added)

Sometime later, they were gathered again. Peter and John had just faced their first opposition as they proclaimed Jesus. They were taken before the Sanhedrin, the Jewish Ruling Council and were told to stop preaching in the name of Jesus. After being released, they went back to the other believers and reported what had happened. Together they entered into earnest prayer asking God for the boldness to continue in the face of the threats. Again, Luke records the dramatic answer to their prayers: "After they prayed, the place where they were meeting was shaken. And they were all *filled with the Holy Spirit* and spoke the word of God boldly" (Acts 4:31, emphasis added). The same people were gathered together—and the outcome was the same; they were all *filled with the Holy Spirit.*

The word used here is the same form of the verb used in Acts 2:4 when they were filled the first time. Accordingly, we must acknowledge that a person can be filled at least twice. It seems clear, however, that God's intention is for this to be a continuing experience. Paul admonished the Ephesian Christians to "not get drunk on wine, which leads to debauchery. Instead, be filled with the Spirit" (Eph. 5:18). The verb form here is a present imperative, which conveys continuing action and would be literally translated as "Keep on being filled with the Spirit."

My long-time friend, mentor, and overseer Harold Bauman suggests a different image to help us understand being *filled with the Holy Spirit,* one that may be especially appropriate given that in both Old Testament Hebrew *(ruach)* and New Testament Greek *(pneuma),* the same word is used for both wind and spirit:

> The word *filled* suggests a container. Perhaps more appropriate is the picture of sails filled with the wind. When the sails are filled, the boat is empowered to action. When the sails are empty, there is deadness, no action. When fullness comes, things happen which could not otherwise happen.[2]

What, then, can we conclude from all this? First, when we are convicted by the Holy Spirit of our sin and our need for God and decide to submit our kingdom to his, we are *born again* with a new spiritual birth, by the living presence of the Holy Spirit in our human spirit.

Second, God's intention for us is that we continually submit our will to that of the Holy Spirit and are carried along by the wind of the Spirit as it "blows wherever it pleases" (John

3:8). This can also be described as being immersed in the river of God's presence and allowing it to carry us along toward the ever-increasing manifestation of his kingdom.

Come, wind of the Spirit, and blow upon us! Come, river of God, and carry us along by your power! Only as this happens will we be "transformed into his likeness with ever-increasing glory, which comes from the Lord, who is the Spirit" (2 Cor. 3:18).

This now brings us to the third of our three phrases, a question raised by the jailer guarding Paul and Silas in the jail at Philippi. It may well be the most widely used—and misunderstood—of the three.

3. What Must I Do to be Saved?

About midnight Paul and Silas were praying and singing hymns to God, and the other prisoners were listening to them. Suddenly there was such a violent earthquake that the foundations of the prison were shaken. At once all the prison doors flew open, and everybody's chains came loose. The jailer woke up, and when he saw the prison doors open, he drew his sword and was about to kill himself because he thought the prisoners had escaped. But Paul shouted, "Don't harm yourself! We are all here!"

The jailer called for lights, rushed in and fell trembling before Paul and Silas. He then brought them out and asked, *"Sirs, what must I do to be saved?"*

They replied, "Believe in the Lord Jesus, and you will be saved—you and your household." Then they spoke the word of the Lord to him and to all the others in his house. At that hour of the night the jailer took them and washed their wounds; then immediately he and all his family were baptized. The jailer brought them into his house and set a meal before them; he was filled with joy because he had come to believe in God—he and his whole family. (Acts 16:25-34, emphasis added)

To persons who have learned the "Just Believe Gospel" discussed in Chapter Two, the most important question to ask someone is "Are you saved?" And, generally, anyone who has prayed "the sinner's prayer" is considered saved.

Sometime back, my wife and I hosted an Alpha Course in our home.[3] I was excited because there were two individuals in the group whose lifestyle was anything but Christian—just the kind of people Alpha was designed for. We had a great time going through the course, but neither one was interested in any kind of new commitment to Christ. Why? Because they were both already "saved." They had already prayed the "sinner's prayer" and could see absolutely no reason for anything beyond that. As someone once said, they had received just enough of the gospel to inoculate them against catching the genuine thing! It was so tragic, because each one remained stuck in a very dysfunctional lifestyle. They were missing out on the genuine transformation that could have been theirs.

Certainly Jesus *is* our Savior and *is* in the business of saving us, as Paul writes:

> Do not be ashamed to testify about our Lord, or ashamed of me his prisoner. But join with me in suffering for the gospel, by the power of God, who has saved us and called us to a holy life—not because of anything we have done but because of his own purpose and grace. This grace was given us in Christ Jesus before the beginning of time, but it has now been revealed through the appearing of our Savior, Christ Jesus, who

has destroyed death and has brought life and immortality to light through the gospel. (2 Tim. 1:8-10)

But what does it truly mean to be saved? I invite you to lay aside your preconceptions and look with me in a fresh way at what the Scriptures have to say about this. We will begin with Paul's words to the Romans:

> You see, at just the right time, when we were still powerless, Christ died for the ungodly. Very rarely will anyone die for a righteous man, though for a good man someone might possibly dare to die. But God demonstrates his own love for us in this: While we were still sinners, Christ died for us.
>
> Since we have now been justified by his blood, how much more shall we be saved from God's wrath through him! For if, when we were God's enemies, we were *reconciled to him through the death of his Son,* how much more, having been reconciled, shall we be *saved through his life!* Not only is this so, but we also rejoice in God through our Lord Jesus Christ, through whom we have now received reconciliation. (Rom. 5:6-11, emphasis added)

Notice what this says: we were *reconciled* to God through the atoning work of Christ on the cross, through his *death.* Now that this is true, "how much more...shall we be *saved* through his *life!*" When we trust Jesus as our Lord and Savior, our relationship is immediately restored—we are reconciled. God is now able to save us as his *life* flows into our lives by the Holy Spirit.

It's helpful here to understand that the word we usually translate as "salvation," *soteria,* also means deliverance. Satan's goal has always been to keep us bound up in our sin and unfruitful in our assignments within our "province" of the kingdom. But as John wrote, "The reason the Son of God appeared was to destroy the devil's work" (1 John 3:8). God now begins the work of delivering us from the power of Satan and the practice of sin.

It is clear this is a process, not a one time event, as the Bible uses the word "saved" in all three tenses—past, present and future, as Ralph W. Neighbour, Jr. has pointed out:

> PAST - For it is by grace you *have been saved*, through faith—and this not from yourselves, it is the gift of God. (Acts 2:8, emphasis added)
> We *have been saved* from the *penalty* of sin, as we have already passed from death to life.
>
> PRESENT - For the message of the cross is foolishness to those who are perishing, but to us who *are being saved* it is the power of God. (1 Cor. 1:18, emphasis added)
> We *are being saved* from the *power* of sin, as its hold on us is being broken in an ever-increasing way as we yield ourselves to God and grow in our relationship and in our kingdom walk with him.
>
> FUTURE - Because of the increase of wickedness, the love of most will grow cold, but he who stands firm to the end *will be saved*. And this gospel of the kingdom will be preached in the whole world as a testimony to all nations, and then the end will come. (Matt. 24:12-14, emphasis added)
> We *will be saved* from the very *presence* of sin when Jesus returns and the kingdom of God comes in all its fullness.[4]

Reconciled through his death; saved through his life. As we submit our lives to God, are cleansed from our sins, and are born again of the Spirit, the transformation process is begun. It is continued as we persistently yield to the work of the Spirit in our lives and are immersed in and filled with the Spirit. The Spirit goes to work to save or deliver us from the things that have made us unproductive in our task of reigning with Christ over our "province" of the kingdom. But he doesn't stop there—he also empowers us to reign effectively with Christ.

While the task of transforming our communities and nations may look much greater than that of eating an elephant, God begins this work the same way: One person at a time, God works the transformation that only he can do—and the effect of this spreads throughout our circle of influence and beyond, as it is multiplied through the circles of influence of those we touch.

When we understand this, like Paul, we will each want to "press on to take hold of that for which Christ Jesus took hold of me" (Phil. 3:12). That brings us to the question we must turn to in the next chapter: "How *do* we take hold of what Christ has provided for us?"

Chapter 6

Taking Hold of the Good News

Fight the good fight of the faith. Take hold of the eternal life to which you were called when you made your good confession in the presence of many witnesses.... Command those who are rich in this present world not to be arrogant nor to put their hope in wealth, which is so uncertain, but to put their hope in God, who richly provides us with everything for our enjoyment. Command them to do good, to be rich in good deeds, and to be generous and willing to share. In this way they will lay up treasure for themselves as a firm foundation for the coming age, so that they may take hold of the life that is truly life. (1 Timothy 6:12, 17-19)

Let's suppose someone—who had the bank account to back it up—has written me a check for one million dollars. People would think me foolish if I just put it away in a desk drawer and left it there. They would expect me to take it to the bank, endorse it, and deposit it to my account. Then I could begin to enjoy what that money could provide.

Well, an even more valuable gift *has been* delivered for each of us, a gift that "richly provides us with everything for our enjoyment." When we take hold of this gift, we have "taken hold of the life that is truly life." But in many cases this precious gift is like my hypothetical check—still lying in the desk drawer waiting for someone to take it to the bank and cash it!

Just over 2000 years ago, God sent Jesus to this earth to deliver the good news of the kingdom, as we have seen. Without question, the value of this good news is certain, and exceeds all worldly wealth, "which is so uncertain." It can transform our lives in ways far beyond our human capabilities to transform ourselves. In fact, we *can't* transform ourselves, if we understand transformation as change at the very core of our nature. Only the God who created us can transform at that level.

So why do so many people leave this tremendous gift in the desk drawer? In many cases, they don't really understand the value of the good news that Jesus offers to them—for reasons we have already looked at. Too many times we have offered artificial gospels that may cause people to feel good for a time, but ultimately leave them feeling empty at the core of their being because they realize there has been little or no genuine transformation of life. They have gained "the form of godliness" but not its transforming power. (2 Tim. 3:5).

In other cases, they simply may not know *how* to cash the check. While someone else writes the check—I couldn't, I don't have the resources—I still must act to receive its benefits. I must endorse it and present it to the bank to be cashed or deposited to my account before the million dollars is available for me to spend.

In the case of the good news of the kingdom, God *has* written the check. But to take hold of those resources, we must take action as well.

In Chapter Four, we described the check. In Chapter Five, we discovered how God can connect this check to our lives to produce transformation. In this chapter, we want to make sure everyone knows how to cash the check—how to take it to the bank and deposit it to our account. Specifically, we will look at how to take hold of the good news of the kingdom and of the Lord Jesus Christ.

Asking the Right Question

As I have listened to people talking to others about cashing the check, the question most often asked is, "Have you been saved?" For me personally, I have decided not to ask that question anymore, even though it is biblically-based, as we have seen. It's just that in our day I'm not sure it is a helpful question. There are far too many people around who are "saved"—meaning they, at some point, "prayed the sinner's prayer"—but there has been virtually no transformation evident in their lives. If they are "saved," there is certainly little *conversion* that has happened, as nothing seems to have turned around in their lives.

Besides, as we saw in the last chapter, the Bible uses "saved" in all three tenses: past, present, and future. It may be a better question to ask, "How are you currently being saved?" That would address the present work of God in a person's life.

As I moved away from asking, "Have you been saved?", I started asking, "Have you been converted?" Now I have come to the place where I think it is better not to single out any one phrase, as it tends to focus our attention on that aspect of the process and misses the others.

Today, I simply ask people, "Have you considered and have you taken hold of the good news that Jesus offers?" If they are interested, I will engage them in a discussion of what I have shared with you in this book. I'm not suggesting this is the only way to talk to people about their response to the good news of the kingdom. I am merely attempting to make sure we are presenting the genuine gospel to people—the one that will transform their lives *and* secure their future.

How, Then, Do We Take Hold?

With the previous chapter as our backdrop, we are ready to ask the central question of this chapter: *How, then, do we "cash the check" and take hold of Jesus and the gospel of the kingdom?* To answer this question, we will note six biblical words and one phrase, as follows:

The Essentials of Salvation
1. Hear
2. Believe
3. Receive

The Evidence of Salvation
4. Repent
5. Confess
6. Turn

The Confirmation of Salvation
7. Be Baptized

The Essentials of Salvation

1. Hear

> But how can people call for help if they don't know who to trust? And how can they know who to trust if they haven't heard of the One who can be trusted? And how can they hear if nobody tells them? (Rom. 10:14, *The Message*)

The first step in taking hold of the good news is hearing the truth of God's word—the truth that God is our friend, not our enemy; that Jesus loves us and gave himself for us; that we can be set free from our sin, our self-centeredness, and from Satan's hold on us; that we can fulfill our God-given destiny of reigning effectively over the sphere of influence God gives us.

We hear the truth of God's word and we hear the convicting voice of the Holy Spirit: "When the Counselor comes, whom I will send to you from the Father, the Spirit of truth who goes out from the Father, he will testify about me" (Jn. 15:26). Many millions of people throughout history have heard God's truth proclaimed, but it rolled off them like water off a duck's back—with no effect. Others have heard and responded in faith. What made the difference? The work of the Holy Spirit in response to what God knew to be in their hearts (Acts 15:8).

Hearing the truth in a way that faith is birthed within us always requires the interaction of God's Word and God's Spirit. Today, we too often have some who are focused almost exclusively on the truth of God's Word, and others focused almost exclusively on God's Spirit. We need the counsel a friend gave me a long time ago:

> The Word without the Spirit, you dry up;
> The Spirit without the Word, you blow up;
> The Word and the Spirit together, you grow up!

2. Believe

> If you confess with your mouth, "Jesus is Lord," and *believe* in your heart that God raised him from the dead, you will be saved. For it is with your heart that you *believe* and are justified, and it is with your mouth that you confess and are saved. As the Scripture says, "Anyone who *trusts* in him will never be put to shame." (Rom. 10:9-11, emphasis added)

Perhaps the most widely known verse of Scripture, John 3:16, says simply, "For God so loved the world that he gave his one and only Son, that whoever believes in him shall not perish but have eternal life." This verse and other similar ones, like Romans 10:9 above, *along with a deep misunderstanding of the word "believe"* have led to the artificial "just believe gospel" discussed in Chapter Two. So what does it mean, biblically, to *believe*?

In today's world, the most prevalent definition of the word is, "to accept as true, genuine, or real."[1] To believe something is to intellectually agree that it is true or real. But to *believe in* God and to *believe in* Jesus means more than that. This is evident in James 2:19—"You believe that there is one God. Good! Even the demons believe that—and shudder." The demons know that God is real, but they will not voluntarily follow him!

Biblically, to believe in Jesus is to *trust* him with your life by submitting to his Lordship. The evidence that to believe is to trust is found in the Romans 10 passage above. The same Greek word, *pisteuō*, appears in this passage three times, and is twice translated as "believe" and once as "trusts."

Further evidence appears in John 2:24. Here many people were gathering around Jesus, excited about the miraculous things he was doing. However, John reports, "But Jesus would not *entrust* himself to them, for he knew all men" (emphasis added). The word is the same. To believe in Jesus is to entrust your life into his hands and follow him in service to the kingdom of God. Persons who have more confidence in their own ability to run their lives than they do in Jesus will never truly follow him in life. They may believe he is real and genuine, but they do not *believe in* him.

I will never forget the powerful illustration of this truth given by my Greek professor, the late Gertrude Roten. She pointed out to us there are two similar prepositions in Greek, *eis* and *en*, both usually translated as "in" in our English versions of the Bible. But *eis* typically conveys "into," while *en* means "in," as in a place: "Believe *in* your heart" (Rom 10:9). When we see "believe in him " or "believe in me," referring to Jesus, the preposition is typically *eis*, rarely another preposition *epi*, meaning "upon," and never *en*.

Therefore, we would literally translate this phrase as "believe into him" or "believe into me." Our English Bibles do not translate it that way because it sounds awkward, but *into* presents a more accurate picture of the real meaning. Professor Roten gave us a graphic image to help us understand the real meaning:

> It's like I'm on the second floor of a burning building and I run to the window and look out. I see Jesus with his arms outstretched towards me and he says, "Jump, and I will catch you." *And I believe into his arms.*[2]

This is a powerful image of what it really means to believe in Jesus—to trust him enough to jump into his arms, trusting him with our very lives. It is simply to rest from our own efforts to save ourselves, and trust the work of Jesus on the cross for our salvation. It is simply to receive God's gracious offer by faith. And that brings us to the next word.

3. Receive

> He was in the world, and though the world was made through him, the world did not recognize him. He came to that which was his own, but his own did not *receive* him. Yet to all who *received* him, to those who believed in his name, he gave the right to become chil-

dren of God—children born not of natural descent, nor of human decision or a husband's will, but born of God. (Jn. 1:10-13, emphasis added)

I *(Jesus)* will rescue you from your own people and from the Gentiles. I am sending you to them to open their eyes and turn them from darkness to light, and from the power of Satan to God, so that they may *receive forgiveness of sins* and a place among those who are sanctified by faith in me. (Acts 26:17,18, emphasis added)

Repent and be baptized, every one of you, in the name of Jesus Christ for the forgiveness of your sins. *And you will receive the gift of the Holy Spirit.* The promise is for you and your children and for all who are far off—for all whom the Lord our God will call. (Acts 2:38,29, emphasis added)

The verb translated as "receive" in these passages is an active word, *lambanō*, rather than a passive one. It means "to reach out and take hold of, to welcome with open arms." In other words, the gifts of God are freely given, but how we receive them is up to us.

As we can see in the passages above, there are three things we receive when we put our trust in Jesus. First of all, we receive forgiveness for our sins. The weight of shame and guilt is taken from us, and we have a new freedom in Jesus. Second, we receive Jesus into our lives as our Lord and Savior. We welcome him into our lives with open arms, to take charge of our lives. Third, we receive the Holy Spirit to empower us, guide us into truth, and endow us with the spiritual gifts needed to fulfill our service to the kingdom of

God—to reign effectively with Christ in that part of the kingdom delegated to us.

Hear, believe, and receive. It really is that simple. And yet, there is one thing that we must note. How do we know when we have really trusted him, and not just prayed a prayer that someone suggested, hoping for something magic to happen? Praying a prayer does not necessarily mean someone has truly put their trust in Jesus. As I was working on some of these thoughts several years ago, I sensed the Spirit saying, "Some people think they have prayed a prayer of faith when they haven't. They have just repeated a mantra."

The Bible is very clear. To receive Jesus as Lord and Savior means a change in lifestyle. The change is empowered by the Holy Spirit, not by one's own self-effort. Yet, if no change becomes apparent, then the person is likely living in deception rather than in salvation.

Now the question becomes, "How do we know we have taken hold of the genuine gospel that transforms, and not just been deceived?" Again, we find three key words in the Scriptures that give evidence a genuine transformation is under way.

The Evidence of Salvation

4. Repent – We change what we think

> Repent therefore and be converted, that your sins may be blotted out, so that times of refreshing may come from the presence of the Lord... (Acts 3:19)

We have already looked extensively at the word for repentance, *metanoia*, meaning "a change of mind." Paul pleads with the Romans to "be transformed by the renewing of your mind" (Rom. 12:2). I love the way Eugene Peterson has paraphrased this passage in *The Message* so much that it has become the theme verse of our ministry:

> Don't become so well-adjusted to your culture that you fit into it without even thinking. Instead, fix your attention on God. You'll be changed from the inside out. Readily recognize what he wants from you, and quickly respond to it. Unlike the culture around you, always dragging you down to its level of immaturity, God brings the best out of you, develops well-formed maturity in you.

We have much too often done exactly what Paul admonished the Romans not to do! We *have* become so well-adjusted to our culture—modern or postmodern—that we have fit into it without even thinking. But as we fix our attention on God, we *will* be "changed from the inside out." Our thinking will change, becoming God-centered rather than human-centered like the culture around us. This is clear evidence that God is at work and his transforming work at the deepest level of our being is under way. Thank God for the "times of refreshing that come from the presence of the Lord" as the Spirit renews our minds!

5. Confess – We change what we say

> Therefore God exalted him to the highest place and gave him the name that is above every name, that at the name of Jesus every knee should bow, in heaven and on earth and under the earth, and every tongue *confess that Jesus Christ is Lord,* to the glory of God the Father. (Phil. 2:9-11, emphasis added)
> If we claim to be without sin, we deceive ourselves and the truth is not in us. If we *confess our sins,* he

is faithful and just and will forgive us our sins and purify us from all unrighteousness. (1 Jn. 1:8,9, emphasis added)

As our minds are changed and renewed, our speech follows suit. The word for "confess" is *homologeō*, meaning literally, "same word." To confess something is simply to say what God says about it. God says "Jesus is Lord," so we say, "Jesus is Lord." This is the "good confession" Paul wrote about to Timothy as he admonished him to "Fight the good fight of the faith. Take hold of the eternal life to which you were called when you made your good confession in the presence of many witnesses" (1 Tim. 6:12).

To confess is the opposite of denial. When we violate a command of God in attitude or action, we are called by Scripture to "confess our sin." That is, we agree with God that this is a violation of his will and his word. Too often, under the influence of our culture, we tend to say, "But you don't understand. That's just the way I am because of how my parents treated me when I was a child." That is either an excuse or denial—or both—but it is *not* confession.

Because neither modernism nor postmodernism recognize God's revealed truth, there is little or no understanding of sin as "missing the mark" any more. And it follows that there is little or no confession of sin. We may admit something as a mistake or an error in judgment, but rarely do we hear people admitting anymore, "This is what I did and this is sin. I confess this and I repent of it."

We have come to believe that the way we deal with our sin is to ask God to forgive it. But that is not the biblical pattern. Biblically, the way we deal with our sin is to confess it and repent of it—to acknowledge it, change our mind about it, and turn and go a different way. As we do this, God forgives us.

This is why many Christians today are still carrying around a lifetime's worth of baggage: they have not followed God's instructions, but instead are begging God to do something he is eager to do, but only on his terms, not ours:

> Repent! Turn away from all your offenses; then sin will not be your downfall. Rid yourselves of all the offenses you have committed, and get a new heart and a new spirit. Why will you die, O house of Israel? For I take no pleasure in the death of anyone, declares the Sovereign LORD. Repent and live! (Ezek. 18:30-32)

This brings us to the third evidence that we have taken hold of the genuine gospel and are being transformed by the power of God.

6. Turn – We change what we do

> First to those in Damascus, then to those in Jerusalem and in all Judea, and to the Gentiles also, I preached that they should repent and turn to God and prove their repentance by their deeds. (Acts 26:20)

As we fix our attention on God, he begins to change the way we think. Our change in thinking leads to a change in our speaking—we begin to agree with God. And as this happens God begins to transform our day-to-day lives—we begin to see changes in what we are doing.

When we see these three things happening in us or in others, we can rest assured that God is at work. Only he can do this at a heart level. On the surface, people can become religious and conform to a different set of rules for a time. But what is inside will come out, sooner or later.

When Jesus was taken to task by the Pharisees and the teachers of the law who accused him and his disciples of eating with "unclean" hands, he replied:

> What comes out of a man is what makes him 'unclean.' For from within, out of men's hearts, come evil thoughts, sexual immorality, theft, murder, adultery, greed, malice, deceit, lewdness, envy, slander, arrogance and folly. All these evils come from inside and make a man 'unclean'. (Mk. 7:20-23)

Come Lord, and transform us! Change our hearts, our thoughts, our words, our actions! As we see this in ourselves, we will be encouraged to press in even harder to the transforming Presence of God. As we see it in others, we will celebrate with them God's work in their lives.

The Confirmation of Salvation

7. Be Baptized

> Then Jesus came to them and said, "All authority in heaven and on earth has been given to me. Therefore go and make disciples of all nations, baptizing them in the name of the Father and of the Son and of the Holy Spirit, and teaching them to obey everything I have commanded you. And surely I am with you always, to the very end of the age." (Matt. 28:18-20)

> Peter replied, "Repent and be baptized, every one of you, in the name of Jesus Christ... (Acts 2:38)

> For we were all baptized by one Spirit into one body—whether Jews or Greeks, slave or free—and we were all given the one Spirit to drink. (1 Cor. 12:13)

Just before Jesus returned to heaven following his resurrection, he told his disciples to go and make disciples of all nations and to baptize them. On the day of Pentecost, when the Church was birthed, the people who heard the message proclaimed by the apostles were convicted of their sin and said, "What should we do?" Peter's response was, "Repent and be baptized, every one of you..."

Being baptized in itself has never saved or transformed anyone. Salvation is birthed and transformation is begun when we, in faith, put our trust in Jesus. However, Jesus instructed his disciples to baptize those they would lead to him.

Baptism is an act of confirmation by the person being baptized, and by the church, that a person has been born again into the kingdom of God. It is a public way of saying, "I have answered the call of Jesus to 'Come, follow me!' I have died to my old self with him, have been buried with him, and have been raised to new life with him! I am now free to reign with him in his kingdom, ordering my life and my sphere of influence after the principles of that kingdom." It is saying before God and the church what Jesus said one day in the home of a tax collector named Zacchaeus, "Today salvation has come to this house..." (Lu. 19:9).

There is another aspect of baptism that often gets overlooked. When we are born again by the Spirit of God, Paul writes that we are "all baptized by one Spirit into one body." As we have already seen, the literal meaning of baptize is to immerse. Thus, we can see this as the Holy Spirit immerses us into the church, into the body of Christ, the family of God. We do not lose our individual identity, but we are no longer alone; we are part of a community of faith, committed to Christ and to each other.

As noted in Chapter Three, my favorite definition of the church is *an outpost of the kingdom*. One of the churches for which I serve as overseer has a large banner hanging in front of their worship center declaring their mission statement: "Visibly Demonstrating the Kingdom of God."

When the church is functioning as God intended, each member has submitted his or her sphere of influence to the kingdom of God and is now reigning with Christ in that "province" of his kingdom. Our individual provinces make up a larger province, called the local church. Together, as each member is faithful to God's call and in reigning with Christ, the local church truly becomes an outpost of the kingdom that visibly demonstrates the kingdom of God. As local churches in a given region work together cooperatively to become a regional province of the kingdom, entire communities will take notice. And transformation will spread—far beyond our expectations!

Dallas Willard captures this reality with the following words:

> Only as we find that kingdom and settle into it can we human beings all reign, or rule, together with God. We will then enjoy individualized "reigns" with neither isolation nor conflict. This is the ideal of human existence for which secular idealism vainly strives. Small wonder that, as Paul says, "Creation eagerly awaits the revealing of God's children."[3]

This is what the artificial cultures of our world long to see—but they are frustrated in their efforts to make it happen because they have cut themselves off from the only One who has the power to make it real.

A Moment of Truth

We have been presented with an overview of the kingdom of God—and how it is an alternative primary culture to the artificial cultures of our world today. We have defined the good news of the kingdom and of the Lord Jesus that the early church proclaimed—and have noted the artificial gospels that abound today. We have seen how God connects the good news to our lives in a way that produces transformation. And we have looked at how we may take hold of this good news.

Now I must ask the question: "Where do you stand regarding all we have discussed?"

- HEAR – Have you heard the truth of God's Word about the good news of the kingdom of God and the Lord Jesus? Well, if you have read to this point, you have! Have you also heard the convicting voice of the Holy Spirit saying, "Yes!" to this truth and birthing faith within you?
- BELIEVE – Have you "believed into Jesus," trusting your life into his hands, submitting your kingdom to his, so that your life and your sphere of influence become a "province" of the kingdom of God? Have you pledged a change of allegiance from self to Jesus as Lord of your life, committed to living as he would live if he were in your shoes?
- RECEIVE – Have you received forgiveness for your sins and been "born of the Spirit" as you trusted Jesus as your Savior? Have you trusted Jesus as the Baptizer with the Holy Spirit, welcoming the Holy Spirit into every part of your life? Have you received the gifts he wants to give you to equip you for effective service in the kingdom of God?
- REPENT – Have you begun to experience a "change of

mind?" Are you finding yourself beginning to think differently, like God thinks, according to his Word? Are you finding your thoughts being fixed on God, rather than being "so well-adjusted to your culture that you fit into it without even thinking?"

- CONFESS – Are you finding that your speech is changing? Are you saying what God says—that Jesus is Lord, and sin is sin? Are you finding your way out of denial and speaking truth?
- TURN – Has there been a turning in your behavior? Are you finding your daily life beginning to change? Is your change of mind and your change of speech becoming visible in a change of behavior? Have you and others around you begun to note this change with excitement and thanksgiving?
- BE BAPTIZED – Have you been baptized, confirming your commitment to Jesus and his kingdom? Have you been immersed into the church as a part of the family of God, the body of Christ committed to carrying out his mission upon this earth?

When we can honestly answer "Yes!" to these questions, then the evidence says we have taken hold of the good news of the kingdom and the Lord Jesus. It also means we "are being transformed into his likeness with ever-increasing glory, which comes from the Lord, who is the Spirit" (2 Cor. 3:18). We have taken hold of a great blessing! It is time to celebrate—and to pass it on.

Blessed to be a Blessing

"I will bless you...and you will be a blessing." (Gen. 12:2) These words, part of God's call to Abraham, are some of the most important words of all Scripture. They convey to us the basic nature of the kingdom of God. God calls us, blesses us—and it overflows to others!

Several years ago I was in a Bible study where these words to Abraham were referred to as a promise and an obligation, or command. Sometime later, I was driving along in my car one day with this passage on my mind, and I clearly sensed God saying to me, "Check it out; you will find it is a statement, not a command." When I got home, I got out my Hebrew Bible and grammar, but I was too rusty to figure it out.

So I called the Hebrew professor at the seminary I had attended and asked him, "Is that a statement or a command?"

"It's a statement," he replied.

Another clear sign that we have taken hold of the gospel of the kingdom is that we feel deep within us the desire to pass on the blessing. In fact, the blessings of God *cannot* be held in—they will naturally overflow to others. If we try to hold on to them, they turn to dust in our hands. Jesus confirmed this as a fundamental principle of God's kingdom with these words:

> If anyone would come after me, he must deny himself and take up his cross daily and follow me. For whoever wants to save his life will lose it, but whoever loses his life for me will save it. (Lu. 9:23,24)

God's salvation and all his blessings are designed to be passed on to others. There are many ways to do this, depending on the "province" of the kingdom assigned to us and the gifts the Spirit gives to us. Again, Jesus himself sets forth some examples:

> Then the King will say to those on his right, 'Come, you who are blessed by my Father; take your inheritance, the kingdom prepared for you since the creation of the world. For I was hungry and you gave me something to eat, I was thirsty and you gave me something to drink, I was a stranger and you invited me in, I needed clothes and you clothed me, I was sick and you looked after me, I was in prison and you came to visit me.'
>
> Then the righteous will answer him, 'Lord, when did we see you hungry and feed you, or thirsty and give you something to drink? When did we see you a stranger and invite you in, or needing clothes and clothe you? When did we see you sick or in prison and go to visit you?'
>
> The King will reply, 'I tell you the truth, whatever you did for one of the least of these brothers of mine, you did for me.' (Matt. 25:34-40)

Another very important means of passing on the blessing is sharing the good news of the kingdom and the Lord Jesus with others. This way, they too may come to faith in Christ and "may take hold of the life that is truly life" as we saw at the beginning of this chapter. We can help them recognize the value of the "check" that has been written out for them—and help them take it to the bank.

In the next chapter we will look at a different paradigm for sharing this good news of the kingdom with others.

Chapter 7

Sharing the Good News With Others

If anyone is in Christ, he is a new creation; the old has gone, the new has come! All this is from God, who reconciled us to himself through Christ and gave us the ministry of reconciliation: that God was reconciling the world to himself in Christ, not counting men's sins against them. And he has committed to us the message of reconciliation. We are therefore Christ's ambassadors, as though God were making his appeal through us. We implore you on Christ's behalf: Be reconciled to God. (2 Corinthians 5:17-20)

But you will receive power when the Holy Spirit comes on you; and you will be my witnesses in Jerusalem, and in all Judea and Samaria, and to the ends of the earth. (Acts 1:8)

There is a remarkable story found in the sixth and seventh chapters of Second Kings. Ben-Hadad, king of Aram (Syria), had come up to the city of Samaria and laid siege to it.

The siege lasted so long that a great famine occurred, as they could get no food into the city. It got so bad that some of the people even resorted to cannibalism. It was a dreadful time. There were four men with leprosy that sat at the gate to the city. They recognized that times were desperate, that they had nothing else to lose, and so they said to each other:

> Why stay here until we die? If we say, 'We'll go into the city'—the famine is there, and we will die. And if we stay here, we will die. So let's go over to the camp of the Arameans and surrender. If they spare us, we live; if they kill us, then we die. (2 Ki. 7:3,4)

That evening they got up and went to the camp of the Arameans. To their amazement, as they arrived in the camp, they found it completely deserted! God had sent the sound of a great army into the camp ahead of them, and the entire Aramean army had left the camp as it was and ran for their lives.

These four starving lepers entered the first tent and found all the supplies left there when the army deserted the camp. They ate and drank their fill and then began to carry out of the tent silver, gold, and clothing that had been left behind. They hid these things, entered a second tent, and again carried off the things left there and hid them as well.

At this point, the realization of what was happening dawned on them—here they were, gorging themselves and carrying off the bounty, while all the inhabitants of Samaria were still in the city dying of starvation. They said to each other, *"We're not doing right. This is a day of good news and we are keeping it to ourselves"* (7:9).

They went back to the city at once and reported what they found. The king sent out some men to confirm what the lepers reported and found it to be exactly as they had said. At that point, the people went out and plundered the camp of the Arameans, and the city was again well-fed and safe.

The Ministry and Message of Reconciliation

When people find genuine good news—like the hypothetical check of the previous chapter, or the food and supplies of the Aramean camp in the story above—the right and healthy thing to do is to share this good news with others. But sometimes people don't share. They may fail to share because they fear the supply will run out, that there is not enough for everyone. Or they may yield to greed, the desire of our old, fallen nature to keep more...and more...and more for ourselves.

When we discover the good news of the kingdom and the Lord Jesus, we have found the greatest news of all. And God's supply is limitless—there is plenty for everyone. So why would Christians fail to pass on this good news—especially since we know the nature of God's blessings is that they must be passed on, lest they dissipate. We are "blessed to be a blessing," as we saw in the previous chapter.

The normal life of a Christian is to pass on the blessings of God to others. It's only when we revert to the selfish influence of our old nature or to the deceit and intimidation of the devil that we are tempted to keep the blessings to ourselves. This is particularly true when it comes to sharing the good news of the kingdom and the Lord Jesus. The devil will do anything to divert people from sharing this message because it is the message of his defeat.

But this message is also the center of our calling as followers of Jesus. "God was reconciling the world to himself in Christ." The disconnect between the upper and lower story that leads to the fragmentation of life was overcome in this great act of reconciliation carried out "in Christ." And now, we have been given both the "ministry of reconciliation" and the "message of reconciliation." In fact, "We are therefore Christ's ambassadors, as though God were making his appeal through us."

The Fallacy of the Gift of Evangelism

There is no indication in Paul's statement above that "we" means only a few who have the "gift of evangelism." Every indication is that it refers back to the "anyone who is in Christ" in verse seventeen. "Anyone who is in Christ" is "Christ's ambassador" and God is "making his appeal through us."

Somewhere we have gotten the idea there is a small number of people—an elite group—that has the "gift of evangelism," and it is only this group that is charged with the task of "sharing the good news." It's true there are three references to "evangelist" in Scripture. Phillip is referred to as "the evangelist" in Acts 21:8. Timothy is charged by Paul to "do the work of an evangelist" (2 Tim. 4:5). And Paul lists "evangelist" as one of the five ministry gifts Christ left with the church when he ascended back to heaven (Eph. 4:11). However, the purpose of these five ministries is outlined in the next two verses:

> To prepare God's people for works of service, so that the body of Christ may be built up until we all reach unity in the faith and in the knowledge of the Son of God and become mature, attaining to the whole measure of the fullness of Christ. (Eph. 4:12,13)

Persons ordained by God to function in these five ministry gifts are not called to pass on the blessings of God *for us*; they are called *to equip all of us* to effectively pass on God's blessing in our "province" of the kingdom, our sphere of influence, "the field God has assigned to us" (2 Cor. 10:13). As we are equipped to function according to our passion and gifting, we will all become effective witnesses and ambassadors of Christ. And all of this will be built around *the ministry and message of reconciliation.* This is the good news of the kingdom of God and the Lord Jesus Christ.

Once, when speaking of the devil, Jesus said, "When he lies, he speaks his native language, for he is a liar and the father of lies" (Jn. 8:44). The devil is a master of half-truths. He loves to take a little truth and then twist it, subtract from it, or add to it. But remember, *a half-truth taken in its entirety is a whole lie.* It is *true* that when Jesus left this earth to return to the Father, he endowed the church with the ministry gift of evangelist. It is *not true* that the ministry and message of reconciliation is now left in the hands of about 10% of the church who have "the gift of evangelism," the other 90% being exempt from sharing the good news of the kingdom in word and deed. To this, *all* who are *in Christ* are called.

Let's look at some different ways of fulfilling this calling. First, we will examine a current model which has contributed to the state of unfruitfulness we currently see in the church, where many people are "saved" but few either converted or truly transformed. Then, I will suggest a biblical paradigm which I believe can help increase our fruitfulness. We will see lives genuinely transformed as people take hold of the genuine gospel, the good news of the kingdom of God.

The Sales Paradigm
This idea that only about 10% of believers are called to pass on the blessing of the good news of the kingdom is one reason we are not expanding the borders of God's kingdom effectively. Another contributing factor is the way that many within this 10% go about it.

The most prominent paradigm, or model, for sharing the good news with others in our day can best be described as the sales paradigm. Or perhaps we should say the *old* sales paradigm, because there is a lot of talk today about a *new* sales paradigm, focused on selling *solutions* rather than products or *commodities*.[1] Actually, the latter seems to be much more compatible with the paradigm I will propose later than does the old one.

In the old sales paradigm, the salesperson is pushing a product, and is trained to go for closure, to make the sale—now! Whether the potential customer really understands the product or not, your job is to make a great pitch that he can't refuse. It's really about the salesperson and his or her ability to make a sale, rather than what the customer needs.

The old sales paradigm for passing on the blessing of the good news of the kingdom is very similar. There is a salesperson attempting to sell a product to a potential customer. The product is "salvation," meaning forgiveness for one's sins and a secure spot in heaven when you die. The salesperson is completely convinced of the need the potential customer has for the product—which is true. But does the *customer* understand that?

As we have seen in Chapter Two, this approach ends up reducing our salvation to two events: First, when a person prays the sinner's prayer, and second, when he or she dies and goes to heaven. And often, the person has no idea how their decision connects to life between those two points. George Barna's research points this out:

> Because the Christian faith is not associated in people's minds with a comprehensively different way of life than they would lead if they were not Christian, the impact of that faith is largely limited to those dimensions of thought and behavior that are obviously religious in nature.[2]

In other words, their faith impacts their religious life—they attend church at least occasionally—but they have no understanding of "a comprehensively different way of life." Most of life is lived just like their non-Christian neighbors.

Another similarity between the old sales paradigm and the way the gospel has been presented is in the push for closure—making the sale. Many times our motivation has been right: This person needs Jesus in their life. And yet, because our focus is on the product, "salvation," we want to see them saved—and now! So we get them to pray the prayer, often before they have a clue what it is all about. They mouth the words of the prayer we lead them in—and then we set to work to assure them of their salvation.

I am convinced that sometimes we are actually countering the work of the Holy Spirit, who is saying to the person, "Wait a minute, do you understand what you are doing? I want to enter into a lifelong relationship with you." By this time, we have moved on to all the "assurance of salvation" scriptures, because we have already made the sale—they have prayed the prayer.

We press for closure because we have heard the words, "But what if they don't pray the prayer and they go out and get hit by a train tonight?" Well, what if we lead them in saying words they don't understand—a kind of mantra— and they leave having no understanding of what it means to live in a relationship with Jesus? *Then* they go out and get hit by a train. Will the words they "prayed" get them into heaven? Friends, if we believe this, then I fear that our faith is in magic, rather than trusting God and his grace with our very lives.

More promising is a *new* sales paradigm offering *solutions* rather than products. That's a step forward as a model for passing on the blessing of the gospel of the kingdom. Here, the focus becomes helping people find a solution to life's problems, for now and for eternity, rather than offering a commodity called "salvation" for the price of a "prayer." And yet, I believe there is an even *better* paradigm. Perhaps it's time to "repent"—to change our minds and think some new thoughts about how people come to faith in Christ and join the journey to transformation.

Thinking New Thoughts
My friend and co-laborer in the kingdom, Ron Klaus, first called my attention to the marriage paradigm as a biblical model for passing on the blessing. Throughout this book, we have noted that the gospel of the kingdom is about living in a relationship with Jesus and serving the kingdom of God in all of life. It is significant for us then that this relationship with Jesus is pictured in the most intimate union—the marriage relationship.

John the Baptist referred to Jesus as the "bridegroom," and to himself as the "the friend who attends the bridegroom" (John 3:29). When Jesus was asked why his disciples did not fast, he replied, "How can the guests of the bridegroom mourn while he is with them? The time will come when the bridegroom will be taken from them; then they will fast" (Matt. 9:15).

Paul gave instructions to husbands and wives by using the analogy of Christ and the church:

> For this reason a man will leave his father and mother and be united to his wife, and the two will become one flesh. This is a profound mystery—but I am talking about Christ and the church. (Eph. 5:31,32)

In The Revelation, John saw the church as the Holy City, the new Jerusalem—the bride of Christ:

I saw the Holy City, the new Jerusalem, coming down out of heaven from God, prepared as a bride beautifully dressed for her husband. And I heard a loud voice from the throne saying, "Now the dwelling of God is with men, and he will live with them. They will be his people, and God himself will be with them and be their God. (Rev. 21:2,3)

It is clear the marriage paradigm is a valid way of describing the relationship between Christ and his church, the people of God. And if that is true, why not think in these terms as we share the gospel with others—as an invitation to a life-long relationship rather than a "sales" event?

The Marriage Paradigm

It has been thirty years since Dr. James Engle's book *What's Gone Wrong With the Harvest?* was first published.[3] In this book, Dr. Engle first presented The Engle Scale. More clearly than before, The Engle Scale helped us understand salvation as a process. It identified 22 typical stages a person moves through on the journey—from first becoming aware of the supernatural but with no knowledge of Christianity, to a mature faith functioning within the body of Christ.

By using the marriage paradigm, we accomplish essentially the same thing. Moreover, we use language that anyone can identify with and understand. As we consider this model, let us first identify the five stages of a marriage relationship:

1. INTRODUCTION – A relationship begins when the parties are introduced and are attracted to one other. The journey towards transformation begins when people are introduced to Jesus.

2. COURTSHIP – Next, these two persons enter a period of courtship. They learn more about each other. In the transformation process, persons get to know more about Jesus and consider if they want to see this relationship continue and grow.
3. ENGAGEMENT – The engagement period begins when both persons decide they want to commit their futures to each other. They make a statement of their intention to marry. Likewise, from the kingdom perspective, persons decide they want to commit themselves to Jesus as Lord and Savior.
4. THE WEDDING – Finally comes the wedding day when their intentions are carried out. They make a public commitment. Baptism is the transformational equivalent—a public "marriage to Jesus," in the context of the family, the church.
5. MARRIED LIFE – The wedding day is the first day of married life. Now the couple begins to live out their covenant relationship on an everyday basis and grow in their love for each other. In the same way, new believers begin to live out their relationship with Jesus, growing towards maturity and fruitfulness in service to the kingdom of God.

Now, let's take a closer look at each of these steps along the way. To illustrate this paradigm, I will use a concrete example—the process by which I entered into a lifelong relationship with my wife, Gwen.

I must say in advance that analogies are seldom, if ever, perfect, and this is no exception. For example, it was seventeen months from the time I first met Gwen until we were married. That does not mean it should normally take seventeen months for persons to move from first being introduced to Jesus until being baptized as a believer. In many cases it will take much less time—sometimes it will take more. I do believe, however, that this paradigm will prove to be helpful to us in developing a healthy model for passing on the blessing of the good news of the kingdom.

1. Introduction

As a college sophomore in early 1968, I was in the middle of a real down time in my life. To begin the year, my grandmother, who had lived with our family all my life, passed away in the middle of January, exactly five months from her 100th birthday. Her death was immediately followed by the end of the first semester, which I finished with the lowest grades of my life—and with little motivation to begin another term.

But the biggest blow was yet to come. I had been dating a girl for almost two years; a relationship that I knew was not a very healthy one. In the middle of a telephone call one evening, my thinking became clear about this—and I jumped in my car, drove to her house, and ended the relationship. Even while I took the initiative and knew it was the right thing to do, emotionally it was a downer.

My cousin and fellow college student, Helen, decided I needed a lift in life, and she had just the solution: I needed to meet Gwen, a fellow nursing student and friend of hers. For two weeks I resisted her attempts to get us together. Then one evening, she invited my roommate and me to the apartment she shared with another cousin of mine to play cards. As soon as I accepted, she went to get Gwen, who was just as excited about meeting me as I was about meeting her!

We spent the evening playing cards, and when it was time to go home, Helen "discovered" she had "lost her keys," so I ended up taking Gwen home in my roommate's 1960 Cadillac—the one with the BIG fins on the back! As I returned to my room, it occurred to me that I had actually enjoyed the evening. So, a week later I accepted an invitation to go bowling with Helen and several of her friends—including Gwen. And as they say, the rest is history!

In the previous chapter, we said taking hold of the good news begins with hearing the truth. In writing the words above, it suddenly became clear there is often, if not always, a previous step: *someone prays.* Paul wrote to the Corinthians, "the god of this age has blinded the minds of unbelievers, so that they cannot see the light of the gospel of the glory of Christ, who is the image of God" (2 Cor. 4:4). It's like there is a cloud over the minds of unbelievers "so that they cannot see the light of the gospel." I doubt if this cloud ever lifts without someone interceding for the person.

In my case, there is no question in my mind that the prayers of my mother led to the opening of my eyes during that fateful telephone call. The cloud of confusion and indecision lifted, and I was able to take action. I knew for a long time that my mother had been praying for me, because she did not want to see me getting serious with a person who was not a Christian. She prayed for me rather than trying to talk me out of the relationship; she knew I was not in a frame of mind to listen.

The combination of Mother's prayers and the respectful persistence of my cousin resulted in my introduction to Gwen. And as we got to know each other, we were drawn to each other. Likewise, the intercession and respectful persistence of a good friend are a powerful combination for introducing people to Jesus and the good news of the kingdom.

Would I have heeded the words of a stranger who thought I needed to meet someone? Possibly, but not likely. Because I knew and trusted my cousin, it was much easier to hear what she was saying. We find the same thing to be true as we share the good news of the kingdom—people who know us and trust us will find it much easier to hear us. This makes the building of solid relationships with non-believers an important part of reaching out with the message of reconciliation.

As people are introduced to Jesus, the Holy Spirit goes to work to draw people to the Father (Jn. 6:44). This opens the door to the next phase of the marriage paradigm.

2. Courtship

Because we felt drawn to each other, Gwen and I began to see each other more frequently as time passed. Over the course of the next year, we spent a lot of time together. We talked about our common faith in Christ. We shared with each other our hopes and dreams for the future. We got to know each other's families. Our trust in each other grew and our relationship deepened. We *understood* each other better. Soon it would be time to "pop the question."

In like manner, when persons are introduced to Jesus and find they are drawn to the Father, they begin to spend more time with God. They read the Word of God and begin to discover God's hopes and dreams for them. They get to know God's family better. Their trust in God's character deepens. They begin to *understand* the call of Jesus to "Come, follow me!" They are moving toward the next phase of the marriage paradigm.

3. Engagement

The day finally came when I was sure that I wanted to spend the rest of my life with Gwen as my wife. I think she was beginning to wonder if I would ever get around to asking the question. I did. She said "Yes!" And so we were engaged. It was our clear intention to follow through with a wedding, when we would officially begin married life.

During the period of engagement, we met several times with the pastor who would marry us. His purpose in this was to make sure we were prepared for the step we were about to take, when we would say, "I take you to be my wife (or husband), from this day forward, for better for worse, for richer for poorer, in sickness and in health, to love and to cherish, and to be faithful to you alone, till death us do part." He wanted to be sure in his mind, before he publicly pronounced us husband and wife, that we *understood* what we were doing and were truly committed to each other.

The equivalent of engagement in the process of a person entering into an intimate, eternal relationship with God comes when persons have an encounter with God and invite Jesus to take charge of their lives as their Lord and Savior. It is a clear statement of intention, as they pray and invite Jesus in.

Is the person "saved" at this point? Would they go to heaven if they died? The answer—as unsatisfying as it may be—is that we don't know. The regeneration of the human spirit in a new spiritual birth is the work of the Holy Spirit. God knows when this happens, but we don't. Why do we need to—unless we are more concerned about taking credit for someone being saved than we are about finding out if a genuine transformation has begun?

Only if our faith is in a formula can we give someone "assurance of salvation" at this point. An evangelist friend of mine came to this realization several years ago. He said to me, "We used to say 'John got saved last night.' Now we say, 'John prayed to receive Jesus last night.' Now we will see if he has been saved."

The truth we must face is that many, many people have come to this point, prayed the prayer of engagement—only to end up like the two persons in our Alpha group, stuck in a very dysfunctional and sinful lifestyle, all the while totally convinced they were Christians. Let's stop "assuring" people of something we don't know for sure is true and risk confirming them in their sin. Why not rather celebrate their engagement, their statement of intent, and then help them prepare for a wedding and a lifetime of faithful and fulfilling married life with their Bridegroom. As the fruit of transformation becomes evident, then we can say with confidence, "God has been at work here! There has been a new birth into God's kingdom. Praise the Lord!

4. The Wedding
I don't remember the date my wife and I were engaged. I do remember the day we were married. At 2:00 p.m. on Sunday afternoon, July 20, 1969, we were married in the Idaville Church of God in the small town of Idaville, Indiana.

Two hours later, we were trying to conduct a reception on the front lawn at Gwen's parents' house, while many of our guests were crammed into the living room watching the *second* most important thing that happened that afternoon—the landing of Apollo 11 on the moon! We watched Neil Armstrong take his "one small step for a man, one giant leap for mankind" from our honeymoon hotel later that night. It seemed to take him forever to get off that ladder!

In this analogy, baptism is the equivalent of the wedding. Just as a wedding is the public celebration of two persons' commitment to each other, so baptism is the public celebration of a person's commitment to Jesus as Lord, Savior, and King. In the wedding, the bride and groom repeat their marriage vows to each other. In baptism, new believers, who are part of the bride of Christ, speak their baptismal vows to Jesus, the bridegroom.

On their wedding day, the bride and groom officially become part of each other's family—a daughter-in-law or son-in-law. Likewise, in baptism the new believers celebrate their entrance into a *new* family—the family of God. Only here they are not in-laws, but full daughters and sons of God.

5. Married Life

While a wedding *is* a time to celebrate, the wedding day is just the first day of married life. I don't remember much about our wedding except the Apollo 11 landing—and our ring bearer picking up all the flowers that our flower girl dropped! But I *do* have a wealth of memories from the more than 36 wonderful years of life we have spent together since then. We also share the expectation that our best years are still ahead of us.

It's a sad reality that often young couples put excessive time, energy, and money into the wedding and little effort into married life. The extravagant cost of the wedding can put such a financial burden on the couple or on their family that it becomes a hindrance to their married life.

To be sure, baptism is a significant event and a time to celebrate. Of *greater* value, however, is the everyday experience of living life in the context of a loving relationship with God in service to his kingdom. Better than any religious formula or isolated event, this life is the treasure we have to share. It will also be the subject of our concluding chapter.

Now is the Time

This is a day of good news. As Paul wrote, "*Now* is the time of God's favor, *now* is the day of salvation" (2 Cor. 6:2, emphasis added). Some of us have been holding this in, afraid of being rejected if we tried to share it with others.

May we all come to the realization the four lepers of Samaria came to as they ate and drank in the Aramean camp: "We're not doing right. This is a day of good news and we are keeping it to ourselves... Let's go at once and report this..." This is the ministry and message of reconciliation—the good news of the kingdom and the Lord Jesus. Let's share it effectively that others may find the integrated life and experience *shalom!*

Chapter 8

Good News for Daily Living

Like newborn babies, crave pure spiritual milk, so that by it you may grow up in your salvation, now that you have tasted that the Lord is good. (1 Peter 2:2)

"We can become like Christ by doing one thing—by following him in the overall style of life he chose for himself. If we have faith in Christ, we must believe that he knew how to live....Spiritual growth and vitality stem from what we actually *do* with our lives, from the *habits* we form, and from the *character* that results." (Dallas Willard[1])

Our adopted son, Christian, was diagnosed early in life with "failure to thrive" syndrome. This was *before* he suffered severe brain damage from being dropped on his head on a concrete floor at six months of age. Children who are neglected and not given the attention they need often suffer from "failure to thrive." They simply fail to grow and develop normally. In some cases it is because they are not given adequate nourishment. In others, the nourishment is adequate, but they do not receive enough love and attention.

The same thing is true of spiritual newborns. If they receive inadequate nourishment or inadequate social interaction and love from others, they will suffer from "failure to thrive." They need the daily nourishment of truth from God's Word and they need loving attention from the family of God. Ensuring that these needs are met in a way which enables spiritual newborns to both survive and thrive is the subject of this chapter.

In order to thrive, however, we must understand and overcome those patterns of thought and behavior running counter to the life of God in us. For those of us who have become believers in adulthood, the following discussion will be of particular importance.

The Power of Habits

My friend Wally Fahrer first introduced me to what he called "The Lazarus Principle" several years ago. In the account of Jesus raising Lazarus from the dead found in John 11, Jesus arrived at the home of Lazarus and his sisters, Mary and Martha, four days after Lazarus had been placed in his tomb. Jesus told the people gathered around to take away the stone from the entrance, and then called out with a loud voice, "Lazarus, come out!" Lazarus came out with the burial linens still wrapped around him. Jesus then said, "Take off the grave clothes and let him go" (Jn. 11:44).

Wally said, "Isn't it interesting that Jesus chose not to unwrap him, but asked his friends to do that? The one who could speak life into the midst of death could certainly have unwrapped him, but he didn't. He left that for his friends to do."

We can make two applications from this story to our own lives. First, when we are birthed by the Holy Spirit into new life in the kingdom of God, we often come in with "grave clothes" from our old life. Second, we need the help of other Christ-followers to get free of them.

Grave Clothes

I believe the "grave clothes" we typically bring with us into the kingdom are unhealthy *habits* formed by sinful lifestyles—both our own and others. What is a habit?

> A recurrent, often unconscious pattern of behavior that is acquired through frequent repetition; an established disposition of the mind or character; customary manner or practice; an addiction.[2]

Sinful thought patterns and actions are habit-forming in themselves. The more they are repeated, the more they become a part of us—and the more they are a part of us, the less we are conscious of it. Then, our unhealthy reactions to the guilt and shame we experience from our own sin, and to the hurt we experience from the sins of others, have free reign to influence and reinforce our habits.

Repeated thoughts lead to repeated actions. Repeated actions become habits—and they are powerful things. C.S. Lewis captured the reality of these "grave clothes" in his book, *The Screwtape Letters*. If you are unfamiliar with the book, "Uncle Screwtape" is the devil and "Wormwood" is an apprentice demon. At one point, Uncle Screwtape is taking Wormwood to task for allowing his "patient" to become a Christian. But he also realizes there is still a force working on their behalf:

> I note with displeasure that your patient has become a Christian...There is no need to despair; hundreds of these adult converts have been reclaimed after a brief sojourn in the Enemy's camp and are now with us.

All the *habits* of the patient, both mental and bodily, are still in our favor.[3]

Without question, old habits have reclaimed many persons who have attempted to walk out a new profession of faith in Christ. It's also true that old habits have severely reduced the effectiveness of many others who are still in the church.

How do we overcome old habits? Thomas à Kempis (1380-1471) gave us the answer to that question many years ago: "Habit overcomes habit"[4] Old habits can only be replaced with new ones. Paul set forth this principle when he wrote, "live by the Spirit, and you will not gratify the desires of the sinful nature" (Gal. 5:16). Only as we develop new habits through the power of the Holy Spirit will we successfully shed our old grave clothes.

How, then, do we "live by the Spirit?" We follow in the footsteps of Jesus, who was "full of the Holy Spirit" (Lu. 4:1). Jesus said, "Anyone who has faith in me will do what I have been doing. He will do even greater things than these, because I am going to the Father" (Jn. 14:12). If we are to do the things that Jesus did, we must live the lifestyle he lived. It was this everyday, disciplined life that prepared him for the times of great ministry that he experienced. We must follow him in this if we expect to follow him in ministry.

The Spiritual Disciplines

In the very first sermon I preached, I quoted from one of my favorite Christian writers, D. Elton Trueblood. Unknown to me, one of his former students was in the congregation. After the service he introduced himself to me and asked, "Would you like to meet Dr. Trueblood sometime?"

"Of course," I replied.

The next week I received a letter from Dr. Trueblood inviting me to come to Richmond, IN where he lived and served as a Professor Emeritus at Earlham College. As others learned of my invitation, everyone wanted to go with me! As an alternative, we invited Dr. Trueblood to come spend a day with us at our church in Indianapolis. He came, preached in the morning service and then we had a sack lunch together and spent a good part of the afternoon sharing. It was one of the most memorable times of my life.

Sometime later I had lunch with one of my professors at the Bible College I was attending and shared with him some of the things I learned from Dr. Trueblood concerning spiritual disciplines. To my great surprise and dismay, he laughed and said, "Don't you understand this is the age of grace?"

To set discipline and grace in opposition to each other is to totally misunderstand both. It is to confuse God's grace with what Dietrich Bonhoeffer called "cheap grace."[5] It is to see grace as permission to stay the same, rather than the power of God to change us into his image. It is to see discipline as legalism and bondage, rather then the doorway to freedom. No athlete will ever be free to perform in the Olympics apart from the consistent practice of discipline. No Christian will ever be free to fulfill their calling to reign effectively with Christ in his kingdom without following him in the spiritual disciplines he practiced.

Spiritual disciplines are activities undertaken "to bring us into more effective cooperation with Christ and his kingdom... to make us capable of receiving more of his life and power without harm to ourselves or others."[6] They are a vital part of keeping our lives integrated, of keeping the upper and lower stories—the spiritual and the physical realms—together.

More then anything else, the failure of Christians to stay integrated in this way has produced the present state of the church:

> *Whatever is purely mental cannot transform the self....* One of the greatest deceptions in the practice of the Christian religion is the idea that all that really matters is our internal feelings, ideas, beliefs, and intentions. It is this mistake about the psychology of the human being that more than anything else divorces salvation from life, leaving us a headful of vital truths about God and a body unable to fend off sin.[7]

This should be sobering to all of us who are part of the body of Christ. Harold Bloom's observation of this failure to keep life integrated is what led him to conclude that much of what passes for Christianity today is really Gnosticism. Integration of life and transformation always go together.

In this book, we can only offer a brief introduction to the spiritual disciplines. If this introduction whets your appetite for more, I recommend *The Spirit of the Disciplines: Understanding How God Changes Lives*, by Dallas Willard.[8] This book was immensely helpful to me.

Willard divides the spiritual disciplines into two categories: disciplines of abstinence and disciplines of engagement.[9] In the disciplines of abstinence, we are saying "no" to the pressures of our old nature and of the prevailing culture, to make room in our lives to say "yes" to the disciplines of engagement. In this way we engage the transforming work of the Holy Spirit.

To practice the disciplines of abstinence is to heed the words of Peter: "Dear friends, I urge you, as aliens and strangers in the world, to abstain from sinful desires, which war against your soul" (1 Pet. 2:11). Paul captures both the disciplines of abstinence and engagement in his admonition to "put off" and "put on":

You were taught, with regard to your former way of life, to *put off your old self*, which is being corrupted by its deceitful desires; to be made new in the attitude of your minds; and to *put on the new self*, created to be like God in true righteousness and holiness. (Eph. 4:22-24, emphasis added)

We must always put our emphasis on the disciplines of engagement. If we major in abstinence, we end up hard, legalistic, religious people. If we recognize the need for abstinence to make room for engagement, *but major in the disciplines of engagement*, we will see the transforming power of the Holy Spirit released in our lives.

Practicing the spiritual disciplines is not jumping through hoops to become a spiritual giant. It is not something we do to manipulate God into doing what we want. It is not building up a bank account in heaven. It is not magic. It is simply part of answering the call of Jesus to "Come, follow me!" It is developing the lifestyle that actually sets us free of our old grave clothes so that we are free to thrive, following Christ in his kingdom.

Following Jesus in the Disciplines

Throughout this book, we have said the call of Jesus has always been, "Come, follow me!" As we follow Jesus in the spiritual disciplines that he practiced, we will walk in the Spirit as he walked in the Spirit. Let's look at some of these and learn from our Lord.

Worship and Service

A. W. Tozer wrote that Jesus came to this earth "in order that he might make worshipers out of rebels."[10] And, as usual, he himself set the pattern for our worship.

To worship is simply to ascribe worth, as David did to God: "Ascribe to the LORD, O mighty ones, ascribe to the LORD glory and strength. Ascribe to the LORD the glory due his name; worship the LORD in the splendor of his holiness" (Ps. 29:1,2). This Jesus did in a myriad of ways, perhaps summed up best in his own prayer to Father God in John 17:4, "I have brought you glory on earth by completing the work you gave me to do." Throughout his life, Jesus showed proper respect and honor to Father God by seeking him out, listening, and then following what he heard and saw.

Paul captured this essence of worship in Romans 12:1, which is expressed in a delightful way in Eugene Peterson's paraphrase, *The Message*: "So here's what I want you to do, God helping you: Take your everyday, ordinary life—your sleeping, eating, going-to-work, and walking-around life—and place it before God as an offering." This is what Jesus did, and this is how we practice the discipline of worship in our lives as well.

This is not to deny that we worship God as we sing our songs of worship during a "worship service." Psalm 100 is a classic example of a psalm of praise and worship:

Shout for joy to the LORD, all the earth.
Worship the LORD with gladness; come before him with joyful songs.
Know that the LORD is God. It is he who made us, and we are his; we are his people, the sheep of his pasture.
Enter his gates with thanksgiving and his courts with praise; give thanks to him and praise his name.
For the LORD is good and his love endures forever; his faithfulness continues through all generations.

I enjoy the privilege of gathering together as the body of Christ and worshiping in this way as much as anyone else. But it becomes a problem when we see this as the sum total of the discipline of worship, and miss the comprehensiveness of a lifestyle of worship as pointed out above.

This brings us to the close connection between the disciplines of worship and service. As Jesus was tempted by the devil to worship him, he responded, "Worship the Lord your God and serve him only" (Lu. 4:8). And, speaking of himself, he said, "the Son of Man did not come to be served, but to serve, and to give his life as a ransom for many" (Matt. 20:28). Jesus links his life of serving others with the greatest act of sacrificial worship the world would ever see—when, in obedience to the mission the Father assigned him, he would allow himself to be placed on the altar of the cross. There he would pour out his life as a sacrifice for the sins of the whole world.

When worship is understood as a comprehensive lifestyle, then worship and service fit together like two sides of the same coin. Whenever they are separated, we again experience a breakdown between the upper and lower stories of life.

This happened among the people whom the king of Assyria sent to live in Samaria after the Israelites were taken into captivity. They did not know how to worship Yahweh, the God of Israel, in whose land they were now living. And things were not going well for them. This was reported to the king, who then sent one of the priests of Israel back to teach the people how to worship the God of Israel. The end result was "They *worshiped* the LORD, but they also *served* their own gods in accordance with the customs of the nations from which they had been brought" (2 Ki. 17:33, emphasis added). The results of this fragmentation were still found hundreds of years later, as Jesus said to one of the women descended from these people, "You Samaritans worship what you do not know" (Jn. 4:22).

Christians who have been unduly influenced by the artificial cultures that we live among suffer the same fragmentation as that of the Samaritans. They *worship* the Lord but *serve* the gods of the culture, just like their non-Christian neighbors. Their faith impacts only their "religious life," not life as a whole, as we saw in George Barna's research in the previous chapter.

In addressing the Samaritan woman at the well, however, Jesus did not just state the problem: he went on to share good news with her. He clearly stated that a new day of integration between the upper and lower stories of life, the spiritual and the physical, was coming and, in fact, was already here: "Yet a time is coming and has now come when the true worshipers will worship the Father in spirit and truth, for they are the kind of worshipers the Father seeks" (Jn. 4:23). Worship in Spirit (upper story) results in worship *and service* in truth—life lived out in accordance with God's truth in everyday life in this physical world. As we follow Jesus in the disciplines of worship and service, we cultivate the integrated life that he lived.

Study and Meditation

Jesus was obviously a student of the written word of God. When faced with the temptations the devil threw at him, three times he answered, "It is written..." and then quoted scriptures that directly addressed the temptation. Like the Psalmist, Jesus understood the value of the word of God in resisting temptation: "I have hidden your word in my heart that I might not sin against you" (Ps. 119:11).

Both study and meditation need to be part of our discipline of the Word of God. We study to gain knowledge and understanding of God's Word. As Paul prepared to address the subject of spiritual gifts, he wrote, "I do not want you to be ignorant." Ignorance is *not* bliss! To be ignorant of what the Bible teaches is to fail to follow Jesus in life.

We all need knowledge, but we also need *more* than knowledge. Again, Paul captures this truth so well:

> We know that we all possess knowledge. Knowledge puffs up, but love builds up. The man who thinks he knows something does not yet know as he ought to know. But the man who loves God is known by God. (1 Cor. 8:1,2)

In addition to the study of God's Word, we need to meditate on it. In meditating on the Word, we muse deeply on a portion of Scripture until the God behind that Word, the God who *is* love, gets through to us. This keeps life in balance.

As a seminary student, I discovered both faculty and students could generally be placed in one of two groups. For one group, the more they learned, the more impressed they were with *what they knew*. For the other group, the more they learned, the more impressed they were with *what they still had to learn*. Knowledge by itself tends to "puff up." This tendency is offset by the practice of meditation which gets us to the heart of God.

Prayer

Jesus was also a man of prayer. Especially when faced with important decisions, he prayed. The night before he called out the Twelve Apostles, he "went out to a mountainside to pray, and spent the night praying to God" (Lu. 6:12). Facing impending crucifixion, he went to one of his favorite places of prayer on the Mount of Olives, Gethsemane, and poured out his heart before his Father: "If it is possible, may this cup be taken from me. Yet not as I will, but as you will" (Matt. 26:39).

During my first trip to Israel, I was asked to lead our tour group in prayer at Gethsemane, a grove of olive trees, some of which were over a thousand years old. As I began my prayer, I was overcome with the realization that it was *here* that the victory over sin was won. It was carried out the next day on Calvary, but it was in Jesus' prayer here in the Garden the night before that it was settled within him—he would carry out the Father's plan. I was so overcome that I could not finish my prayer.

Too many times we set in contrast things that ought not to be, such as praying and doing. The fallacy of this is clear in a story related to me by one of my professors. The year before I started my seminary studies, some monks from a monastery located nearby came to one of the weekly forums to share about their life of prayer. After their sharing, one of the more activist students asked, "How can you spend so much time praying when there is so much to be done?"

"Sir," the monk replied, "What evidence do you have that your doing is accomplishing more than my praying?"

In prayer and meditation, we hear the voice of the Spirit and know what to do. Otherwise, we are in danger of a life of activity that may look good on the surface yet have little impact for the kingdom of God.

Solitude and Silence

Jesus was also a man who understood the need for solitude and silence: "Very early in the morning, while it was still dark, Jesus got up, left the house and went off to a solitary place, where he prayed" (Mk. 1:35). As we withdraw from the crowds to be alone with God, we find relief from all the clutter and clamor of a society that cannot tolerate quietness.

Why do we find silence so hard? I believe there is a connection between this and the general shallowness of our relationships. As Eberhard Arnold has written, "People who love one another can be silent together."[11] While my wife and I also have times of great conversation, I find it easier to be silent with Gwen than with anyone else. In other relationships that don't share the same depth, it seems I always feel I *must* talk—otherwise, what will people think of me?

As we practice the disciplines of silence and solitude, we open the door for more fruitful prayer and meditation—and for the deepening of our love relationship with God. As Elijah listened for God to speak to him, God's voice came neither in the wind, the fire, nor the earthquake, but in a "gentle whisper" (1 Ki. 19:12). How do we hear a gentle, loving whisper in the midst of a noisy crowd?

Fasting

Jesus was acquainted with the discipline of fasting as well, as he fasted for 40 days during his time of temptation. (Lu. 4:1). Anyone who has attempted fasting knows you don't start with forty days! While we don't read about it in the gospels, it should be obvious that the time of his temptation was not his first experience of fasting.

Fasting is not the same as dieting. We diet to lose weight. We fast for very different reasons. We fast from common bread to feast on the *other bread*—the "bread of life", the "bread that came down from heaven"—Jesus himself. Thus, fasting can be seen both as a discipline of abstinence and one of engagement. We abstain from food and drink to focus on engaging the Holy Spirit in a deeper way.

There is another reason for the discipline of fasting, as well as other disciplines of abstinence. They help us keep things in proper perspective. Food is a wonderful thing—we must have it to survive! Yet, it can take a place in our lives that is not healthy. Paul wrote of those for whom "their god is their stomach" (Phil. 3:19). Fasting is a way of saying with Paul:

> "Everything is permissible for me"—but not everything is beneficial. "Everything is permissible for me"—but I will not be mastered by anything. "Food for the stomach and the stomach for food"—but God will destroy them both. (1 Cor. 6:12,13)

Other disciplines of abstinence mentioned by Willard perform this same function. We just looked at the disciplines of solitude and silence. These help keep us from being mastered by the loudest voice in the crowd. Secrecy keeps us from being mastered by a need for recognition. Frugality keeps us from being mastered by money and things. Sacrifice keeps us from being mastered by the self-focus so common in our culture.[12]

Submission
Jesus also understood the discipline of submission, as he would do "only what he sees his Father doing," and would only "speak just what the Father has taught me" (Jn. 5:19; 8:28). Submission is another one of those biblical concepts, like authority, that has fallen on hard times in our age of autonomy. It's hard for the human self to permit submission to anything other than itself.

But we must define what we mean by submission. Submission is related to, but not the same as, obedience. It is possible to walk in submission without being obedient. The classic example of this is found in Acts, chapters four and five. Peter and John had been called before the Sanhedrin, the supreme authority in Israel, because they had been preaching about Jesus. They were ordered to stop this at once and then released.

Peter and John went right back to the Temple and began to teach the people about Jesus. Again, they were called before the Sanhedrin and asked why they had disobeyed their orders. "We must obey God rather than man," they replied.

They were then flogged and released—a Roman flogging was no minor punishment! They submitted to the flogging and went on their way "rejoicing because they had been counted worthy of suffering disgrace for the Name" (Acts 5:41). Peter and John respected the authority of the Sanhedrin and submitted to their punishment. Yet they refused to obey because they had been called to preach by a higher authority, King Jesus.

On the other hand, it is possible to practice obedience without submission. Submission is an attitude of the heart. Both children and adults sometimes obey authority under the threat of force, while inside they are seething with anger. This is obedience, but not submission. Once the threat of force is removed, they often demonstrate their lack of submission.

In the discipline of submission, we submit to the authority that God places over us, both in the civilian world and in the kingdom of God. In fact, it's in learning to submit to these authorities, particularly as children recognize their parents' authority, that we learn to submit to God.

Concerning loving God, John wrote, "anyone who does not love his brother, whom he has seen, cannot love God, whom he has not seen" (1 Jn. 4:20). I think the same principle can be applied in the area of submission: Anyone who will not submit to earthly authorities that are seen won't submit to the authority of the unseen God either. There are many people today who move from one church to another because they "answer only to God." They are in deception—and in rebellion against those who could train them to submit to God's authority.

Of course, authorities in the kingdom of God are called to follow Jesus in exercising their authority as well—as servants, not overlords. When James and John came to Jesus to request the top positions of authority in Christ's kingdom—at his right and his left—he spoke some very important words to them:

> You know that those who are regarded as rulers of the Gentiles lord it over them, and their high officials exercise authority over them. *Not so with you.* Instead, whoever wants to become great among you must be your servant, and whoever wants to be first must be slave of all. For even the Son of Man did not come to be served, but to serve, and to give his life as a ransom for many. (Mk. 10:42-45, emphasis added)

"Not so with you." With those words, Jesus established a fundamental difference in how kingdom authority functions compared to worldly authority. Kingdom authorities are servants, not overlords. When authorities function this way and the people they serve practice submission, the kingdom of God flourishes. When either party takes their cues from the world rather than the Word, problems arise.

The discipline of submission opens the door for another discipline that Jesus practiced—the discipline of community. Because of the importance of this discipline, and the lack of understanding of it in our day, we will look at this one in greater depth.

The Discipline of Community

We introduced the "Lazarus Principle" addressed earlier in this chapter. We have examined the first application of the "Lazarus Principle," the replacing of the "grave clothes" of old habits through the practice of spiritual disciplines that help us establish new patterns of thought and behavior. Now we will look more closely at the second application, the reality that we cannot do this alone, but need the help of others in this process.

Evaluating his creation, God said, "It is not good for the man to be alone" (Gen 2;18). We were created to be in relationship with others. Of course, here the context is the most intimate of all human relationships, that of husband and wife. But the principle applies across the board: "It is not good for *anyone* to be alone." This stands out clearly in Ecclesiastes 4:9-12:

> Two are better than one, because they have a good return for their work: If one falls down, his friend can help him up. But pity the man who falls and has no one to help him up!
> Also, if two lie down together, they will keep warm. But how can one keep warm alone?
> Though one may be overpowered, two can defend themselves. A cord of three strands is not quickly broken.

Perhaps one of the most often repeated phrases I have heard in the last several years has been, "Christianity is about relationship, not about religion." It is about a relationship with God that opens the door to healthy relationships with others as well. The New Testament word for these special relationships that include God, us, and others is the Greek word, *koinonia*. The word literally means "to share with or participate with." Because we *participate* in the life of Christ (1 Cor. 10:16), we also *share* a special relationship with other followers of Jesus.

Three Levels of Relationships
We experience this *koinonia* on three levels. First, we experience the "fellowship with the Spirit" (Phil. 2:1) with all true followers of Jesus everywhere. In October 1997, I joined approximately one million other men on the National Mall in Washington, D.C. for the Promise Keepers' "Stand in the Gap" rally. I enjoyed this fellowship with a number of other men around me whom I had never seen before and will likely never see again this side of heaven. But because we all shared a relationship with Jesus, we also shared a special relationship as "brothers in Christ" (Col. 1:2) as well.

On the second level, we share *koinonia* with a group of Christ-followers with whom we have an on-going relationship. This may be a group of up to 200, which is about the maximum number we can know on a first name basis. In many cases, this group corresponds to the local church or congregation in which followers of Jesus participate. In larger churches with multiple worship services, this may be the other members of the particular service that we attend.

But there is also a third level on which we experience *koinonia*. This level we will call community. Community is usually experienced in groups of about 15 or less. It is in this setting that we can practice all of the "one-another" passages of Scripture:

> A new command I give you: *Love one another.* As I have loved you, so you must love one another. By this all men will know that you are my disciples, if you love one another. (Jn. 13:34-35)

> *Be devoted to one another* in brotherly love. *Honor one another* above yourselves. (Rom. 12:10)
>
> You, my brothers, were called to be free. But do not use your freedom to indulge the sinful nature; rather, *serve one another* in love. (Gal. 5:13)
>
> Be completely humble and gentle; be patient, *bearing with one another* in love. (Eph. 4:2)
>
> *Be kind and compassionate to one another, forgiving each other*, just as in Christ God forgave you. (Eph. 4:32)
>
> Therefore *encourage one another* and *build each other up,* just as in fact you are doing. (1 Thess. 5:11)
>
> And let us consider how we may *spur one another on* toward love and good deeds. (Heb. 10:24)
>
> Therefore *confess your sins to each other* and *pray for each other* so that you may be healed. The prayer of a righteous man is powerful and effective. (Jas. 5:16, emphasis added in all above)

These verses of Scripture are not pious platitudes to be ignored by Christians because they have better things to do. They are at the core of life lived in the kingdom of God. They are the ways that we help each other grow in our competency to reign with Christ in our "province" of the kingdom. We ignore them to our own loss.

They *are* often ignored by Christians because they have no setting in which to carry them out. These are not the kinds of things that can happen on a consistent basis in a group of 100 people or more. They are a part of community life in a small group of 15 persons or less. Again, let's look at the example Jesus set for us.

Community in the Life of Jesus
As Jesus began his public ministry, large crowds of people began to gather around him. He taught them and ministered to them. These crowds undoubtedly contained both curious onlookers and persons who were serious about following him. This latter group was called his "disciples."

One night Jesus went out to a mountainside to pray and spent the entire night there. Then, "when morning came, he called his disciples to him and chose twelve of them" (Luke 6:13). It was this small group of disciples, also called apostles, that was to spend the rest of his earthly ministry with him. To them, he taught and ministered on a deeper level. After teaching the larger crowds, "when he was alone with his own disciples, he explained everything" (Mk. 4:34). This small group of twelve men formed Christ's new community—the core group of the first church.

It's also clear from Scripture that, within this new community of 12 men, there was an inner circle of three, and included Peter, James, and John. He spent even more time with these three than with the other nine, as a smaller leadership circle. Accordingly, it should be no surprise to hear "Peter and John" mentioned more often than the others in the early days of the church, especially prior to Paul's conversion. It should also not surprise us to see this early church repeating the pattern of smaller groups within a larger group.

Community in the Early Church
William Beckham uses the analogy of a bird to describe the early church. Just as a bird needs two wings to fly, so the early church was a "two-winged church," with one wing for

"large group celebration" and the other for "small group community."[13] This two-winged pattern is clear in Scripture:

> Every day they continued to meet together *in the temple courts.* They broke bread *in their homes* and ate together with glad and sincere hearts, praising God and enjoying the favor of all the people. And the Lord added to their number daily those who were being saved. (Acts 2:46,47, emphasis added)
>
> Day after day, *in the temple courts* and *from house to house,* they never stopped teaching and proclaiming the good news that Jesus is the Christ. (Acts 5:42, emphasis added)

It's equally clear this was not just the Jerusalem pattern, where the early followers of Jesus had access to the temple for larger gatherings. Paul, who ministered in the Gentile cities of Asia Minor, followed this same two-winged approach:

> You know that I have not hesitated to preach anything that would be helpful to you but have taught you *publicly* and *from house to house.* I have declared to both Jews and Greeks that they must turn to God in repentance and have faith in our Lord Jesus. (Acts 20:20,21, emphasis added)

Why this two-winged pattern? To press the analogy, anyone who has seen a bird trying to fly with only one good wing understands the need for both wings. A one-winged bird spends a lot of energy flapping around in a circle without ever getting off the ground.

We need both small and large groups for the same reason. Without both, it's unlikely that our lives in Christ will ever really get off the ground. There are some needs that we have that will not be met in a large group setting. No one has expressed it to me more clearly than my friend Wally Fahrer: "You *inspire* and *inform* in the large group, and you *transform* in the small group."

As a person primarily gifted as a teacher, I can teach the Word of God to a gathering of three people...or 300...or 3,000. And I have never been more inspired in worship than when standing with the one million men gathered on the National Mall, as I mentioned earlier. We can *inspire* and *inform* in the large group.

However, *transformation* happens when truth gets applied to real life in the context of loving relationships. In this context we can practice the "one-another" scriptures mentioned above. We can practice accountability with one another. When we can say to a few close friends, "This is what we want to work on in our lives at this point, and we want you to pray for us and hold us accountable," we have prepared a seedbed for the work of the Holy Spirit.

We must clarify something, however, to keep accountability healthy. *Accountability* is holding people accountable for the decisions they make. *Control* is trying to make the decision for them. When we do this, we are invading their "province" of the kingdom, and are attempting to do something even God will not do.

Keeping Community Healthy

The new community of disciples that Jesus called together found that building community life is not without its trials. We are all imperfect people, works-in-progress, and anytime we get serious about community and accountability, sooner or later our imperfections will show. This was no less true among the Twelve than among us. James and John came to Jesus with a request: they wanted the positions of honor, at Jesus' right and left, when he came into his glory. When the others heard about this, "they became indignant with James and John" (Mk. 10:41).

Whenever a new community forms, we can expect it to go through some recognizable phases of life. The first phase is called "Acquaintance," as people are just getting to know each other. Everyone is happy and excited to be part of the group. Everyone likes everyone else.

But then we get to know each other better—and find that we all have our own little quirks that can be downright annoying to others! And our differing expectations for the group begin to surface. We have entered the second phase of community life, the "Conflict" phase. The temptation at this point is to run. "This group just isn't what I thought it was going to be. I'm going to find another one!" But if we run at this point, what are we going to do when our next group experience ends up like the first?

My friend Jim Egli refers to these first two phases as "Illusion" and "Disillusion." The rosy picture we have of each other during the acquaintance phase is an illusion, not reality. When this dawns upon us, it is easy for feelings of disillusionment to rise up within us. But, as Jim says, if we will just press through this phase of disillusion, we can reach the third phase, that of "Joy," or genuine community.

God is never surprised at our imperfections. That is why he has given us clear guidelines in Scripture for dealing with conflict in constructive ways. If we will be open and honest with each other and keep loving one another, we actually have an opportunity to bring glory to God out of our conflict! We do this as the work of the Holy Spirit becomes evident in our lives in the midst of our conflict. We don't avoid real issues, but we remain respectful of each other.

Ken Sande has genuinely blessed the church with his book, *The Peacemaker: A Biblical Guide to Resolving Personal Conflict*.[14] Few books have impacted my life to the extent that this one has. I highly recommend it to every follower of Jesus. It will help us get over the hump of "Disillusion," and on to "Joy!" as we follow Jesus in the discipline of community.

Thrive, Don't Just Survive!
When Gwen and I were in the process of adopting Christian, some people thought it was very unwise of us, because of his severe brain damage. One doctor who performed a physical for Christian tried to talk Gwen out of the adoption. "He's not going to get better—he's just going to get bigger," he said emphatically. Gwen came home in tears.

"There are three things wrong with that," I said. "Number one, he's not God, he doesn't know that.

"Number two, he *will* get better, either in this life or in eternity. Jesus has paid the price of his healing. We just don't know when.

"Number three, even if he doesn't get better in this life, he deserves a family to love him and care for him."

As I write this, Christian is now eight years old. He still suffers from severe brain damage, and will for his lifetime—apart from a restorative miracle of God. But he no longer has a diagnosis of "failure to thrive."

He has not only survived, he has in many ways thrived. He is growing. He is a happy child, and blesses many lives that he touches with his smiles and his deep laughs.

Our daughter, Destinee, and Christian have blessed us in so many ways. They are a constant, prophetic witness in our home of a generation that God is not finished with. The devil has thrown a lot at this generation. But he has not and will not succeed. Christian—and all those who carry his name—have a Destiny! That's the good news of the kingdom.

As we cultivate the life of the Spirit within us through the spiritual disciplines and through loving relationships, we, too, will thrive as we reign with Christ in his kingdom.

Epilogue

> As God's fellow workers we urge you not to receive God's grace in vain. For he says,
> "In the time of my favor I heard you,
> and in the day of salvation I helped you."
> I tell you, now is the time of God's favor, now is the day of salvation. (2 Corinthians 6:1,2)

If you have made your way through the pages of this book to this point, you likely are either a Christian open to thinking new thoughts, or a seeker open to learning more about the good news that Jesus brought to this earth so long ago.

If you are in this latter group, I trust this book has brought more understanding to you of what it means to reach out and take hold of the good news of the kingdom of God and the Lord Jesus Christ. With Paul, I say to you, "now is the time of God's favor, now is the day of salvation." I sincerely hope that you find, and rest in, that favor.

If you are in the former group, thank you for staying with me as I have challenged some ideas which may be very dear to you. I believe we are in a very critical period in the history of the church. It is a time to think—to muse—not just a·muse with the dominant culture. It is a time to restore the biblical foundations necessary to see transformation come to the church and to our world.

I believe this is where we must begin—with our understanding of the gospel itself. The good news of the kingdom, proclaimed by Jesus and the early church, *is* the good news that transforms. It's the genuine gospel for the increasingly artificial world in which we live. If we take hold of it, we will find that the six needs mentioned in Chapter One are all met in Christ. With Paul, we will find "all the promises of God in Him are Yes, and in Him Amen, to the glory of God through us" (2 Cor. 1:20, NKJV).

I will leave you with two words of encouragement, one from long ago and one more recent.

> God will not destroy without building again. He makes all things new. God knows what He is doing; we must trust Him to pull down and to build up as He will. He does not do these things for no purpose; something great lies hidden under it all. The whole Creation is subject to the will of God and we also, whether we understand what He does or not. He does not need our advice as to what He does. (Jan Comenius, 1660, Amsterdam[1])

> We are at the front edges of the greatest transformation of the church that has occurred for 1,600 years. It is by far the greatest change that the church has ever experienced in America; it may eventually make the transformation of the Reformation look like a ripple in a pond. That transformation is occurring because of the persistent call of God that our whole world be made new, and that the church's mission in that world be itself transformed in new patterns of reconciling the world to God....There are enormous

tasks and daunting challenges for those who intend to follow that call, but then the Lord never said it would be easy. (Loren Mead, 1991, Washington, DC[2])

NOTES

Introduction

1. Peter Cheltschizki, *The Net of Faith*, Bohemia, 1440, quoted in Edmund Hamer Broadbent, *The Pilgrim Church* (Grand Rapids: Gospel Folio Press, 1999), p. 146.
2. Gallup, George Jr., *Religion in America—50 Years: 1935-1985*. The Gallup Report, May 1985, Report No. 236, p.12.
3. George Gallup, Jr. and Timothy Jones, *The Next American Spirituality: Finding God in the Twenty-first Century* (Colorado Springs: Cook Communications, 2000), p. 32f.
4. "transform," *The American Heritage Dictionary*, Electronic Edition, Third edition, Version 3.6p, © 1994, SoftKey International, Inc.
5. Dallas Willard, *The Divine Conspiracy: Rediscovering our Hidden Life in God* (San Francisco: HarperSanFrancisco, 1997), p. 40.
6. Gallup and Jones, p. 15.

Chapter 1: How About Some Good News?

1. George H. Gallup Jr. *1992 Yearbook of American and Canadian Churches* (Nashville: Abingdon Press, 1992), p.
2. "culture." Webster's Third New International Dictionary, Unabridged. Merriam-Webster, 2005. http://unabridged.merriam-webster.com (30 Jun. 2005).
3. Oz Guinness, *Time for Truth: Living Free in a World of Lies, Hype, & Spin* (Grand Rapids, Baker Book House, 2000), p.15.
4. Howard A Snyder, *Liberating the Church: The Ecology of Church & Kingdom* (Downers Grove, InterVarsity Press,1983), p. 120.
5. John R.W. Stott, *Christian Counter-Culture: The Message of the Sermon on the Mount* (Downers Grove, Il: InterVarsity Press, 1978), p. 10.
6. Francis A Schaeffer, *Francis A. Schaeffer Trilogy: The Three Essential Books In One Volume* (Wheaton: Crossway Books, 1990), p. 286.
7. Ludwig Feuerbach, *The Essence of Christianity*, trans. by George Eliot (New York: Harper & Brothers, 1957), p. 270f.
8. "genuine." *The American Heritage Dictionary*, Electronic Edition, Third edition, Version 3.6p, © 1994, SoftKey International, Inc.
9. "artificial." *The American Heritage Dictionary*.
10. Schaeffer, p. 53.
11. Schaeffer, p. 319. Words in italics are my additions.

12. Ravi Zacharias, *The Real Face of Atheism* (Grand Rapids: Baker Books, 2004), p. 79.

13. Sophia Voravong, "Warning Signs There, But Little Was Done, Neighbors Say," *Lafayette Journal and Courier*, March 23, 2005, sec A:8.

Chapter 2: What Is the Good News?

1. A.W. Tozer, *The Best of A.W. Tozer*, ed. Warren W. Wiersbe (Grand Rapids: Baker Book House, 1978), p. 103.

2. Luther's words in Roland H. Bainton, *Here I Stand: A Life of Martin Luther* (New York: Penguin Books, 1955), p. 49f.

3. Dallas Willard, *The Divine Conspiracy: Rediscovering our Hidden Life in God*. (San Francisco: HarperCollins, 1997). See Chapter Two, "Gospels of Sin Management," for a more complete account of this problem.

4. Tozer, p. 103,104.

5. Harold Bloom, *The American Religion*, (New York: Simon & Schuster, 1992), p. 37.

6. Bloom, p. 30.

7. John S. Spong, "A Call for a New Reformation," online article available at <http://www.dioceseofnewark.org/jsspong/reform.html> (11/05/2002).

8. Anne Lamont, *Traveling Mercies* (New York: Pantheon, 1999), p. 41, quoted in George Gallup Jr. and Timothy Jones, *The Next American Spirituality: Finding God in the Twenty-First Century* (Colorado Springs: Cook Communications, 2000), p. 58.

9. Spong, "A Call for a New Reformation."

10. Ibid.

11. Alan Wolfe, *The Transformation of American Religion. How We Actually Live Our Faith* (New York: Free Press, 2003), p. 2f.

Chapter 3: The Kingdom of God

1. The heart of this diagram comes from George Eldon Ladd, *The Gospel of the Kingdom* (Grand Rapids: Eerdmans, 1959). See pp. 24-51. I have expanded it to give further clarity.

2. William A. Beckham, *The Second Reformation: Reshaping the Church for the 21st Century* (Houston: Touch Publications, 1995), p.84.

3. For a fuller discussion of this, see Harley Swiggam, *The Bethel Series, Old Testament* (Madison, Wisconsin: Adult Christian Education Foundation, 1981). See pages 3-17.

4. Alternate reading from the footnote in the NIV

5. John S. Spong, "A Call for a New Reformation," online article available at <http://www.dioceseofnewark.org/jsspong/reform.html>, (11/05/2002).
6. Leslie Stahl interview with Bishop Spong, aired on CBS' "60 Minutes" 5/21/2000, CBS Worldwide Inc.
7. "just." *The American Heritage Dictionary*, Electronic Edition, Third edition, Version 3.6p, © 1994, SoftKey International, Inc.
8. George Eldon Ladd, *A Theology of the New Testament* (Grand Rapids: Eerdmans, 1974), p. 632.

Chapter 4: The Good News of the Kingdom

1. Alan Wolfe, *The Transformation of American Religion : How We Actually Live Our Faith* (New York: Free Press, 2003), p.3.
2. *The Pilgrim Hymnal*, 1904
3. Dallas Willard, *The Divine Conspiracy*, p. 21.

Chapter 5: The Process of Transformation

1. The "Transformations Videos" and other resources that document and address transformation around the world can be found on the website, <www.sentinelgroup.org>
2. Harold E. Bauman, *Presence & Power: Releasing the Holy Spirit in the Life of Your Church* (Scottdale, PA: Herald Press, 1989), p.75.
3. The Alpha Course was developed by Nicky Gumbel at Holy Trinity Brompton Church in London. All Alpha resources are available from their website, <www.alphacourse.org>
4. Ralph W. Neighbour, Jr., *Survival Kit for New Christians: A Practical Guide to Spiritual Growth* (Nashville, TN: Convention Press, 1979). See pages 62-85 for a thorough discussion of these three aspects of our salvation.

Chapter 6: Taking Hold of the Good News

1. "believe." *Collegiate Dictionary.* Merriam-Webster, 2005. http://unabridged.merriam-webster.com/MWOL-home.htm (18 Aug. 2005).
2. This is a very close, if not completely accurate, quote of Professor Roten's illustration, given in Basic New Testament Greek class at the Associated Mennonite Biblical Seminary, Summer 1978. This dear saint has gone to be with the Lord, so I have no way to verify her exact words.
3. Dallas Willard, *The Divine Conspiracy* (San Francisco: HarperCollins, 19 1997), p. 27.

Chapter 7: Sharing the Good News With Others

1. For example, see Sharon Drew Morgan, *Selling With Integrity* (New York: Berkley Books, 1999).

2. George Barna, "Survey Shows Faith Impacts Some Behaviors But Not Others," THE BARNA UPDATE, October 22,2002, <http://www.barna.org/FlexPage.aspx?Page=BarnaUpdate&BarnaUpdateID=123, accessed 03-03-2005>

3. James F. Engle, *What's Gone Wrong With the Harvest: A Communication Strategy for the Church and World Evangelization* (Grand Rapids: Zondervan, 1975)

Chapter 8: Good News for Daily Living

1. Dallas Willard, *The Spirit of the Disciplines: Understanding How God Changes Lives* (San Francisco: HarperCollins, 1988), pp. ix, 20.

2. "habit." The American Heritage Dictionary, Electronic Edition, Third edition, Version 3.6p, © 1994, SoftKey International, Inc.

3. C.S. Lewis, *The Screwtape Letters* (New York: The Macmillan Company, 1951), p.15.

4. Thomas à Kempis, *The Imitation of Christ*, translated by William C. Creasy (Macon, GA: Mercer University Press, 1989), p.23.

5. Dietrich Bonhoeffer, *The Cost of Discipleship*, translated by R. H. Fuller, revised by Irmgard Booth, 2nd edition (New York: Macmillan, 1959), p. 45.

6. Willard, p. 156.

7. Willard, p. 152.

8. I especially recommend chapters eight and nine.

9. Willard, p. 158.

10. In an excerpt from *Worship, the Missing Jewel of the Evangelical Church*, reprinted in *The Best of A .W. Tozer*, compiled by Warren Wiersbe (Grand Rapids: Baker Book House, 1978), p.217.

11. Quoted in Willard, p.165.

12. See Willard, Chapter Nine, "Some Main Disciplines for the Spiritual Life."

13. William A. Beckham, *The Second Reformation: Reshaping the Church for the 21st Century* (Houston: Touch Publications, 1995), p.25.

14. Ken Sande, *The Peacemaker: A Biblical Guide to Resolving Personal Conflict*, Third Edition (Grand Rapids: Baker Books, 2004)

Epilogue

1. Jan Amos Comenius, *Voice of Mourning*, quoted in Edmund Hamer Broadbent, *The Pilgrim Church* (Grand Rapids: Gospel Folio Press, 1999), p. 156.

2. Loren Mead, *The Once and Future Church: Reinventing the Congregation for a New Mission Frontier* (Washington, DC: Alban Institute Publications, 1991), p. 68

BIBLIOGRAPHY

Bainton, Roland H. *Here I Stand: A Life of Martin Luther.* New York: Penquin Books, 1955.

Barna, George. "Survey Shows Faith Impacts Some Behavior But Not Others." *THE BARNA UPDATE.* Oct 22, 2002. Mar 3,2005. <http://www.barna.org/FlexPage.aspx?Page=BarnaUpdate&BarnaUpdateID=123>

Bauman, Harold E. *Presence & Power: Releasing the Holy Spirit in the Life of Your Church.* Scottdale, PA: Herald Press, 1989.

Beckham, William A. *The Second Reformation: Reshaping the Church for the 21st Century.* Houston: Touch Publications, 1995.

Bishop Spong. Prod. Shari Finkelstein. "60 Minutes," May 21, 2000. Videocassette. New York: CBS Worldwide Inc, 2000.

Bloom, Harold. *The American Religion.* New York: Simon & Schuster, 1992.

Bonhoeffer, Dietrich. *The Cost of Discipleship.* Trans. R. H. Fuller, rev. Irmgard Booth, Second Edition. New York: Macmillan, 1959.

Broadbent, Edmund Hamer. *The Pilgrim Church.* Grand Rapids: Gospel Folio Press, 1999.

Engle, James F. *What's Gone Wrong With the Harvest: A Communication Strategy for the Church and World Evangelization.* Grand Rapids: Zondervan, 1975.

Feuerbach, Ludwig. *The Essence of Christianity.* Trans. George Eliot. New York: Harper & Brothers, 1957.

Gallup, George Jr. *1992 Yearbook of American and Canadian Churches.* Nashville: Abingdon Press, 1992.

──────────. *Religion in America—50 Years: 1935-1985. The Gallup Report.* May 1985. Report No. 236.

Gallup, George Jr. and Timothy Jones. *The Next American Spirituality: Finding God in the Twenty-First Century.* Colorado Springs: Cook Communications, 2000.

Guinness, Oz. *Time for Truth: Living Free in a World of Lies, Hype, & Spin.* Grand Rapids: Baker Book House, 2000.

Gumbel, Nicky. *The Alpha Course Manual.* Colorado Springs: Cook Ministry Resources, 1995.

Ladd, George Eldon. *A Theology of the New Testament.* Grand Rapids: Eerdmans, 1974.

————. *The Gospel of the Kingdom.* Grand Rapids: Eerdmans, 1959.

Lewis, C.S. *The Screwtape Letters.* New York: The Macmillan Company, 1951.

Mead, Loren B. *The Once and Future Church: Reinventing the Congregation for a New Mission Frontier.* Washington, DC: Alban Institute Publications, 1991.

Morgan, Sharon Drew. *Selling With Integrity.* New York: Berkley Books, 1999.

Neighbour, Ralph W. *Survival Kit for New Christians: A Practical Guide to Spiritual Growth.* Nashville: Convention Press, 1979.

Sande, Ken. *The Peacemaker: A Biblical Guide to Resolving Personal Conflict,* Third Edition. Grand Rapids: Baker Books, 2004.

Schaeffer, Francis A. *Francis A. Schaefer Trilogy: The Three Essential Books in One Volume.* Wheaton: Crossway Books, 1990.

Snyder, Howard A. *Liberating the Church: The Ecology of Church & Kingdom.* Downers Grove: InterVarsity Press, 1983.

Spong, John S. "A Call for a New Reformation." Nov 5, 2002. <http://www.dioceseofnewark.org/jsspong/reform.htm>

Stott, John R.W. *Christian Counter-Culture: The Message of the Sermon on the Mount.* Downers Grove: InterVarsity Press, 1978.

Swiggam, Harley. *The Bethel Series.* Madison: Adult Christian Education Foundation, 1981.

The American Heritage Dictionary, Electronic Edition, Third Edition, Ver. 3.6p, CD-ROM. SoftKey International, Inc. 1994.

Thomas, à Kempis. *The Imitation of Christ.* Trans. William C. Creasy. Macon, GA: Mercer University Press, 1989.

Tozer, A.W. *The Best of A.W. Tozer.* Ed. Warren W. Wiersbe. Grand Rapids: Baker Book House, 1978.

Voravong, Sophia. "Warning Signs There, But Little Was Done." *Lafayette Journal and Courier.* Mar 23, 2005, sec A: 8.

BIBLIOGRAPHY 197

Webster's Third New International Dictionary, Unabridged. Merriam-Webster. Jun 30, 2005. <http://unabridged.merriam-webster.com>

Willard, Dallas. *The Divine Conspiracy: Rediscovering our Hidden Life in God*. San Francisco: HarperSanFrancisco, 1997.

———. *The Spirit of the Disciplines: Understanding How God Changes Lives*. San Francisco: HarperCollins, 1988.

Wolfe, Alan. *The Transformation of American Religion: How We Actually Live our Faith*. New York: Free Press, 2003.

Zacharias, Ravi. *The Real Face of Atheism*. Grand Rapids: Baker Books, 2004.

ABOUT THE AUTHOR

Dale Stoll served as Senior Pastor at Tri Lakes Community Church in Bristol, IN for 22 years—from 1979 to 2001. Dale and Gwen have been married since 1969 and have five children and six grandchildren. They are also foster and adoptive parents, and have had sixteen foster children over the last fifteen years, two of whom they have adopted.

Dale is the founder and director of Radical Restoration Ministries, LLC (RRM), a ministry of Tri Lakes Community Church birthed in October 2001, growing out of Dale's years of pastoral ministry there. Dale is ordained by and under the spiritual oversight of Teaching the Word Ministries of Leola, PA. RRM is committed to the restoration of radical Christianity in our time.

Dale serves the church through RRM as a teacher, writer, overseer and mentor. He is currently involved in oversight with nine congregations, including Tri Lakes, and is active in leadership of the Michiana Regional Pastors Prayer Network. He also leads the Association of Radical Church Networks (ARC NET).

Dale is a graduate of Purdue University with a B.S. degree in Psychology, and also attended the Associated Mennonite Biblical Seminary for three years.